# GRAPHIC GUIDE
# TO INTERIOR DESIGN

written and drawn by
FORREST WILSON

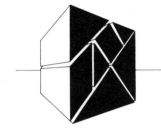

PROFESSOR OF ARCHITECTURE AND CHAIRMAN, DEPARTMENT OF ARCHITECTURE AND
PLANNING, SCHOOL OF ENGINEERING AND ARCHITECTURE, THE CATHOLIC UNIVERSITY
OF AMERICA, WASHINGTON, D. C.

 VAN NOSTRAND  REINHOLD  COMPANY
New York  Cincinnati  Toronto London  Melbourne

UNDERTAKEN AS PART OF DOCTORAL INVESTIGATION IN DEMYSTIFYING AND
POPULARIZING ENVIRONMENTAL DESIGN TECHNIQUES.
UNION GRADUATE SCHOOL

GRATEFUL ACKNOWLEDGEMENT FOR THE CRITICAL ASSISTANCE OF DR. ROY FAIRFIELD,
DR. PEGGY COHN, DR. NORMAN COHN, DR. DIANA MCGARY, AND DR. ARNOLD FRIEDMANN.

for    **BETTY**
jonathan
robert
paul

LIBRARY OF CONGRESS CATALOG CARD NUMBER 76-45280

ISBN 0-442 - 29549-9 (CLOTH)
     0-442 - 29552-9 (PAPER)

PRINTED IN THE UNITED STATES OF AMERICA

PUBLISHED IN 1977 BY VAN NOSTRAND REINHOLD COMPANY
A DIVISION OF LITTON EDUCATIONAL PUBLISHING, INC.
450 WEST 33RD STREET, NEW YORK, NY 10001, U.S.A.

VAN NOSTRAND REINHOLD LIMITED
1410 BIRCHMONT ROAD, SCARBOROUGH, ONTARIO MIP 2E7, CANADA

VAN NOSTRAND REINHOLD AUSTRALIA PTY. LIMITED
17 QUEEN STREET, MITCHAM, VICTORIA 3132, AUSTRALIA

VAN NOSTRAND REINHOLD COMPANY LIMITED
MOLLY MILLARS LAND, WOKINGHAM, BERKSHIRE, ENGLAND


16 15 14 13 12 11 10 9 8 7 6 5 4 3 2 1

LIBRARY OF CONGRESS CATALOGING IN PUBLICATION DATA
WILSON, FORREST, 1918-
   GRAPHIC GUIDE TO INTERIOR DESIGN.
   INCLUDES INDEX.
   1.   INTERIOR DECORATION--HANDBOOKS, MANUALS, ETC.
   2.   DESIGN--HANDBOOKS, MANUALS, ETC.  I.  TITLE.
NK2113.W54      729'.2      76-45280
ISBN  0-442-29549-9
ISBN  0-442-29552-9 PBK.

# CONTENTS

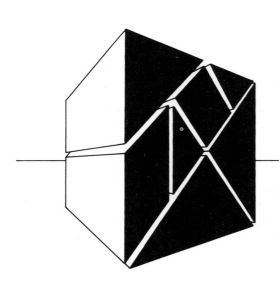

DESIGN IS OFTEN SAID TO BE SUCH A MYSTERIOUS THING THAT ONLY VERY SPECIAL PEOPLE CAN UNDERSTAND IT.  THE PEOPLE WHO SAY THIS ARE USUALLY PROFESSIONAL DESIGNERS.

THIS BOOK IS BASED UPON THE ASSUMPTION THAT DESIGN IS IN REALITY A RATHER SIMPLE ACTIVITY WHICH WE ALL DO EVERY DAY WITHOUT MAKING ANY FUSS ABOUT IT.

TO DESIGN IS TO INTEND, TO MEAN, TO PLAN MENTALLY, TO OUTLINE, AND TO SCHEME, WHICH SEEM ORDINARY ENOUGH ACTIVITIES.  THIS DOES NOT MEAN THAT TALENT, INTUITION, AND INSPIRATION ARE NOT VALUABLE.  THEY ARE, BUT MUCH TOO VALUABLE TO BE USED INDISCRIMINATELY.  INTUITION IS SAVED UNTIL ALL REASONABLE EFFORTS HAVE BEEN MADE TO GAIN KNOWLEDGE AND AFTER ALL RATIONAL WAYS OF USING THAT KNOWLEDGE HAVE BEEN EXHAUSTED.  ART·IS THE PRECIOUS ELEMENT THAT IS INTRODUCED IN ADDITION TO, NOT IN PLACE OF RATIONAL SOLUTIONS.

TO UNDERSTAND A PROBLEM IS TO ACQUIRE THE POWER TO SOLVE IT.  THE MORE WE KNOW, THE MORE DECISIONS WE CAN MAKE AND THE BETTER THEY WILL BE.

CREATIVITY, ORIGINALITY, AND INSPIRATION ARE COMMON ENOUGH HUMAN ATTRIBUTES.  WE CANNOT DO ANYTHING THAT IS NOT BASED ON THE PAST EXPERIENCE OF OTHERS.  THIS IS OUR HUMAN HERITAGE.  ON THE OTHER HAND IT IS IMPOSSIBLE TO EXACTLY DUPLICATE ANYTHING DONE BEFORE WITHOUT ADDING SOME OF OUR OWN IDEAS AND PREFERENCES.  EACH PERSON IS A UNIQUE COMBINATION OF SENSIBILITIES AND EXPERIENCES.  IT IS IMPOSSIBLE NOT TO USE THE IDEAS OF OTHERS AND IMPOSSIBLE NOT TO ADD SOME OF OUR ORIGINAL SELVES TO THEM.

THE PURPOSE OF THIS BOOK IS TO EXPLAIN THE IDEAS OF INTERIOR DESIGN AS A SIMPLE SQUARE.  A SQUARE IS NOT A VERY COMPLICATED GEOMETRIC FIGURE. ALL OF ITS SIDES ARE THE SAME LENGTH AND ALL OF ITS ANGLES ARE RIGHT ANGLES. IT IS SOMETIMES SAID DISPARAGINGLY THAT SIMPLE IDEAS ARE SQUARE.  PERHAPS THEY ARE, BUT BUILDING "TO SQUARE" MEANS TO PLACE ACCURATELY IN POSITION.

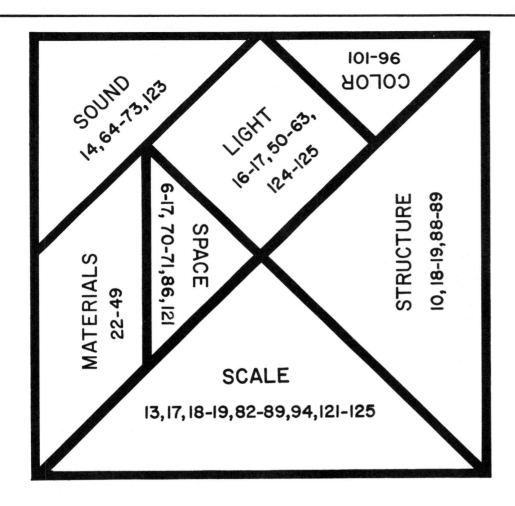

WE CAN THINK OF THE BOOK AS AN ENTITY.  IT DESCRIBES ALL THE ESSENTIAL
ELEMENTS OF THE ACTIVITY THAT WE CALL INTERIOR DESIGN.  ANY ELEMENT OF THE
WHOLE MAY BE ASSIGNED GREATER OR LESSER IMPORTANCE BUT THEY MUST ALL BE CON-
SIDERED IN ARRANGING THE PARTS OF A DESIGN.

ALTHOUGH WE OFTEN HAVE A TENDENCY TO MAKE SIMPLE THINGS COMPLICATED,
WHICH IS CERTAINLY TRUE OF "DESIGN", WE MUST NOT FORGET THAT ONCE THE
ELEMENTS OF A SIMPLE IDEA ARE UNDERSTOOD THEY CAN BE INFINITELY VARIED.

# SPACE

**....** is the designer's material

FORMED BY THE RELATIONSHIP BETWEEN **IT** AND THE HUMAN BEING WHO SENSES IT...

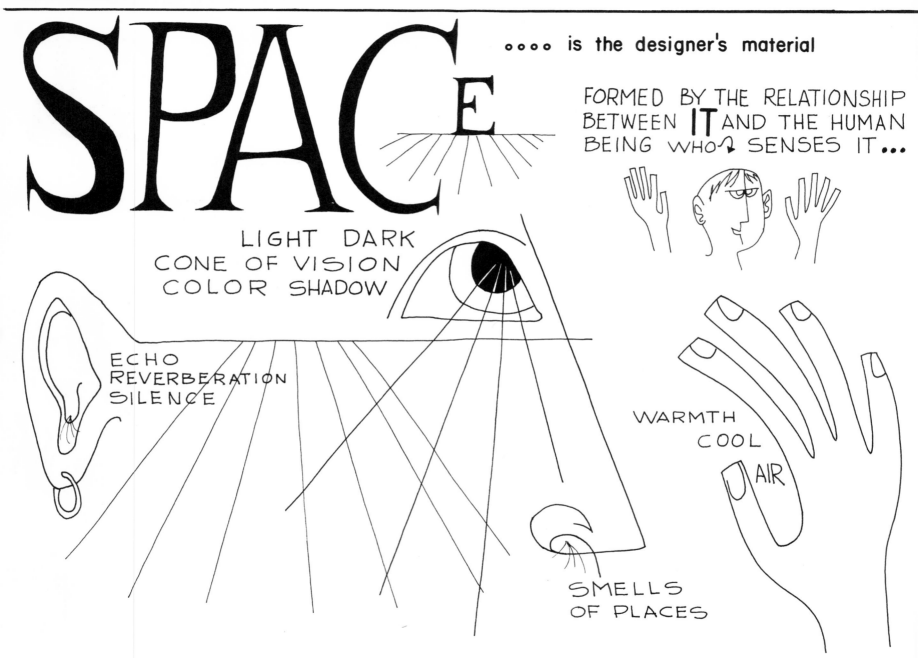

LIGHT DARK
CONE OF VISION
COLOR SHADOW

ECHO
REVERBERATION
SILENCE

WARMTH
COOL
AIR

SMELLS
OF PLACES

DELIMITING EXTERIOR
SPACE – A BIT OF PERSONAL
SPACE IN UNIVERSAL SPACE

EXTERIOR – INTERIOR
SPACE – FLOOR,
COLUMNS, AND ROOF

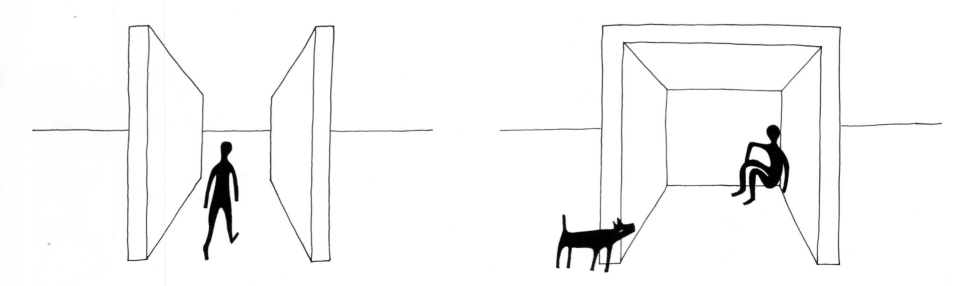

FLOOR AND WALLS
DIRECTING EXTERIOR SPACE

INTERIOR SPACE –
FLOOR, WALLS, AND ROOF

8

BLACK ON WHITE?
WHITE ON BLACK?

HOW DO YOU SEE WHAT
IS NOT THERE?

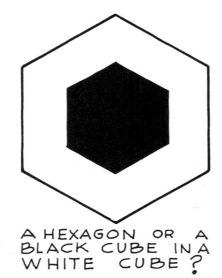

A HEXAGON OR A
BLACK CUBE IN A
WHITE CUBE?

A VASE        THE SPACE
              IN THE VASE

THE EDGES OF STRUCTURES
ARE THE BOUNDARIES OF
SPACE

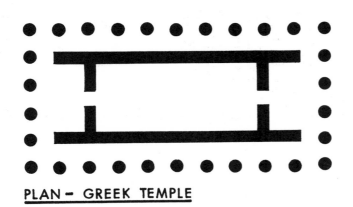

PLAN - GREEK TEMPLE

STRUCTURE ENCLOSING SPACE

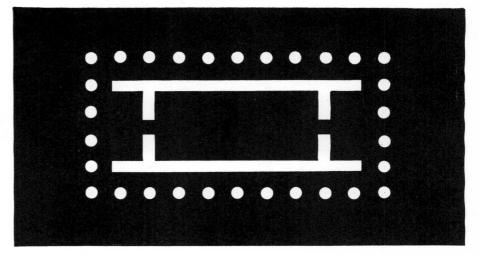

SPACE ENCLOSING STRUCTURE

# STRUCTURE
ONE
TWO
THREE DIMENSIONS

### ONE-LINE

### TWO-PLANE

### THREE-SOLID

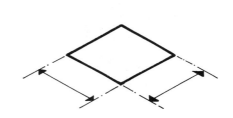

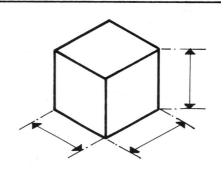

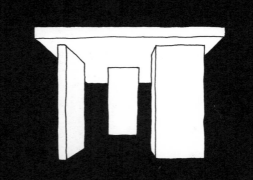

COLUMNS — BEAMS — RAFTERS

EXTERIOR SPACE MIXED WITH

INTERIOR SPACE.  NO CLEAR

DIVISIONS BETWEEN THE TWO.

FLOOR — WALLS — ROOF

EXTERIOR SPACE ENTERS THROUGH

OPENINGS AROUND OR THROUGH PLANES.

SOLID MASS OF FLOOR — WALLS — ROOF

INTERIOR SPACE HOLLOWED FROM SOLID.

INTERIOR SPACE TOTALLY CONTROLLED.

DOORS AND WINDOWS ARE SPATIAL TRANSITIONS
FROM EXTERIOR TO INTERIOR SPACE. THEY CAN
BE IMPORTANT, CASUAL, PROTECTIVE, FLAMBOYANT,
ORDINARY, POMPOUS OR HUMBLE. A LOT IS SAID
ABOUT SPACE INSIDE BY THE DESIGN OF THE
PASSAGES BETWEEN EXTERIOR AND INTERIOR SPACE.

THE LOW ENTRANCE DOORS OF A CATHEDRAL MAGNIFY
THE SPATIAL SENSATION OF THE SOARING INTERIOR
SPACE. THIS BRINGS US TO HOW PEOPLE FEEL THE
GEOMETRY OF THE SPACE THAT SURROUNDS THEM.

# SENSING SPACE

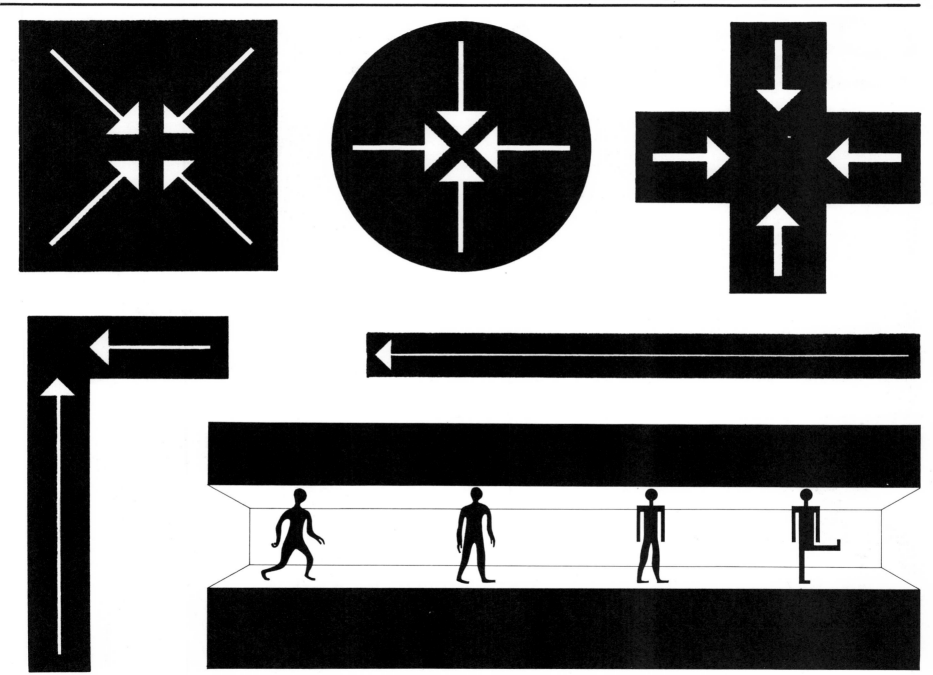

# SONIC SPACE

THE HUMAN EAR DETECTS SMALL VARIATIONS IN AIR PRESSURE THAT
REGISTER SOUND ON OUR EAR DRUMS OVER A BROAD RANGE OF INTENSITIES.
AS SOUND BOUNCES FROM WALLS, FLOORS, AND CEILINGS IT SENDS MESSAGES
WHICH DEFINE INTERIOR SPACE.

WE ORIENT OURSELVES IN SPACE BY LOCATING THE SOURCE OF SOUNDS.
WE INTERPRET ROOM SIZES BY THE REFLECTANCE OF SOUND ENERGY.  SPACE
CAN BE TRANSFORMED BY EXTREME QUIET OR LOUD NOISE.  WE CAN EXPERIENCE
THE SOUND OF A CONCERT HALL AND ITS GREAT SPACES BY PUTTING EARPHONES
ON OUR HEAD EVEN THOUGH WE ARE SITTING IN A CLOSET.

DISTANCE IS JUDGED BY LOUDNESS AND SOUND VOLUME.  SOUND DECREASES
OR INCREASES AS WE APPROACH OR RETREAT FROM IT.  DIRECTIONAL JUDGMENTS
ARE BASED ON THE SOURCE OF NOISE OR CONVERSATION.

IF SONIC INFORMATION IS UNCLEAR, THE LISTENER AMPLIFIES THE
SOURCE OF THE SOUND AMID THE CONFUSION BY FOCUSING ONE EAR AND IGNORES
SOUND JUMBLE RECEIVED BY THE OTHER.

WOW

SOUND FROM THE RIGHT OR LEFT IS
IDENTIFIED BY THE DIFFERENT INTENSITY
REACHING EITHER EAR.  SOUND FROM THE
FRONT, REAR, OR ABOVE AFFECTS BOTH EARS
EQUALLY.  WE TURN OUR HEADS TO FOCUS OUR
EARS TO LOCATE THE SOUND SOURCES.

A SENSE OF THE SURFACE QUALITY OF AN INTERIOR SPACE IS TRANSMITTED BY THE SONIC CLUE OF REVERBERATION. THE COMPOSITION OF ROOM SURFACES AND FURNISHINGS AFFECTS THEIR ABILITY TO TRANSMIT AND RECEIVE SONIC INFORMATION.

WHEN A SOUND SOURCE STOPS ABRUPTLY, CEASING TO EMIT ENERGY, THE REMAINING ENERGY WITHIN THE SPACE CONTINUES TO REFLECT BETWEEN THE ROOM SURFACES. AS SOUND WAVES SUCCESSIVELY PASS THE LISTENER'S EAR, THE ORIGINAL SOUND CONTINUES TO BE HEARD AS IT DIMINISHES IN INTENSITY. ROOM SIZE IS INDICATED BY REVERBERATION TIME.

A ROOM SOFTENED BY UPHOLSTERED FURNISHINGS PROMPTS A DIFFERENT PERCEPTUAL RESPONSE THAN ONE THAT IS EMPTY, WITH HARD UNCOVERED SURFACES.

SONIC SPACE IS CREATED BY LOUD NOISES WHICH DRIVE PEOPLE AWAY FROM ITS SOURCE OR PLEASING SOUNDS WHICH PEOPLE GATHER AROUND TO HEAR.

PEOPLE FEEL THAT THEY HAVE A RIGHT TO SILENCE BUT ABSOLUTE SILENCE IS UNNERVING, EVEN PAINFUL. A LOW SOUND LEVEL, EQUIVALENT TO THE RUSTLE OF LEAVES OR THE LAPPING OF WAVES ON A SANDY BEACH, IS REASSURING.

SOUND CAN PROMOTE PRIVACY. IN A LARGE OPEN OCCUPIED ROOM THE LEVEL OF SOUND OFTEN CREATES ZONES OF PRIVACY WHERE INTIMATE CONVERSATION IS POSSIBLE.

VISUAL SPATIAL CLUES ARE THE STRONGEST AND THEREFORE TEND TO DOMINATE OUR JUDGMENT. BUT OUR SENSUAL REACTION TO SPACE IS ALSO DETERMINED BY SOUND CONDITIONS. SINCE THEY ARE LESS OBVIOUS, THEY ARE OFTEN MORE DIFFICULT TO RECOGNIZE AND CONTROL.

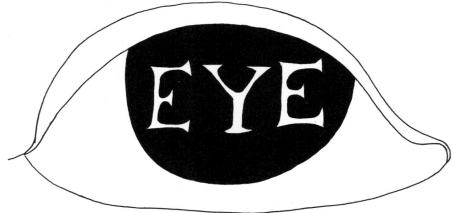

WE SEE CLEARLY IN A VERY SMALL AREA PARALLEL TO THE LINE OF SIGHT. IF WE LOOK DIRECTLY AT AN OBJECT AS SMALL AS A COLON FROM AS LITTLE AS A FOOT AWAY, THE EYE MUST CHANGE POSITION TO FOCUS DIRECTLY ON BOTH DOTS.

OUTSIDE OF A VERY SMALL AREA OF PRECISE VISION THERE IS A BROADER AREA OF PERIPHERAL VISION. IN THIS RANGE OUR PERCEPTION OF DETAIL AND COLOR BECOMES SUCCESSIVELY LESS CERTAIN AS IT MOVES AWAY FROM THE CENTER OF VISION.

THIS PERIPHERAL FIELD CAN BE DEFINED AS A CONE OF APPROXIMATELY 30 DEGREES ABOVE, BELOW, AND TO EACH SIDE OF THE CENTER. WE CAN SEE THINGS RELATIVELY CLEARLY IN THIS AREA. SURROUNDING THIS IS AN AREA OF GENERAL COMPREHENSION EXTENDING ABOUT 60 DEGREES ABOVE AND TO EACH SIDE AND 70 DEGREES DOWN FROM THE LINE OF SIGHT. BEYOND THIS, EXTENDING APPROXIMATELY AT RIGHT ANGLES TO THE LINE OF SIGHT, MAJOR FORMS REGISTER AS INDISTINCT MASSES.

WITHIN THE CENTRAL PORTIONS OF THE FIELD OF VIEW, CHANGES IN BRIGHT-NESS, PATTERN, AND INTENSITY ARE DISCERNIBLE. IN THIS AREA THE EYE IS RELATIVELY SENSITIVE TO FLICKER AND MOVEMENT.

PERIPHERAL VISION INFLUENCES THE ROOM OCCUPANT'S ABILITY TO MAINTAIN A SENSE OF GENERAL ORIENTATION AND A RELATIONSHIP TO THE DYNAMIC ACTIVITIES IN THE SPACE.

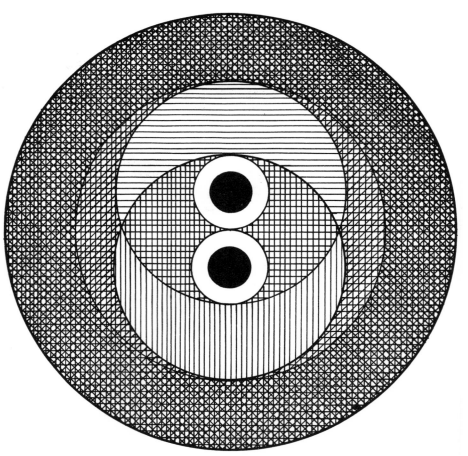

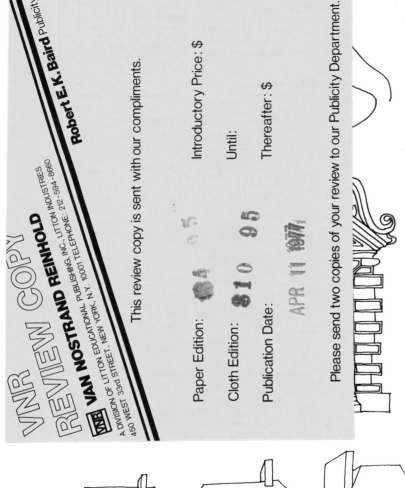
BECAUSE OF THE WAY OUR EYES FUNCTION THERE IS A
GRADUATED SCALE OF DESIGN.  THERE IS THE SCALE OF
ART, WHICH CAN BE VIEWED FROM A DISTANCE OF ABOUT 4
FEET.  THE SCALE OF ARCHITECTURE IS FROM 4 TO 40 FEET
TO VIEW IT IN ITS TOTALITY.  AT THIS DISTANCE THE WORK
OF ART BECOMES A DETAIL.  THEN THERE IS THE SCALE OF
THE CITY, ABOUT 400 FEET, IN WHICH THE BUILDING
BECOMES A DETAIL.

THE SCALE OF INTERIOR DESIGN VARIES FROM THAT OF
ART, WHICH IS THE END OF OUR NOSE, TO THAT OF ARCHITECTURE,
WHICH WE NEVER SEE IN ITS ENTIRETY AT THE SAME TIME.

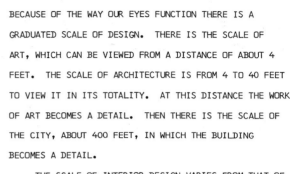

ARCHITECTURE - THE WORK
OF TOOLS  AND MACHINES -
MUST BE  WALKED INTO AND
AROUND  TO BE  SEEN -
VIEWED FROM  4 TO 40 FEET

PLANNING - THE CITY, THE WORK
OF TOOLS  AND MACHINES - MUST BE
VIEWED FROM  AN  AUTOMOBILE OR AN
AIRPLANE TO BE SEEN AT A
DISTANCE OF  40  TO  400 FEET

# GEOMETRY

## THE RANGE OF FORM WITHIN ANY ONE STRUCTURAL FAMILY IS RICH AND VARIED

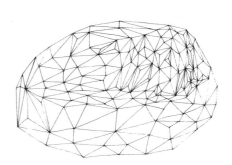

ONE DIMENSION - LINE - SKELETON

TWO DIMENSION - PLANE - SHELL

THREE DIMENSIONS - SOLID - MASS

18

LINE

PLANE

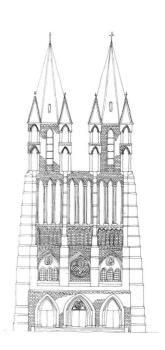

THE WAY MATERIALS REACT TO
THE FORCES APPLIED TO THEM
IN THE THREE FORMS OF
STRUCTURE IS THE BASIS
OF THE DESIGNER'S
FORMAL INSPIRATION

SOLID

ALL BUILDING MATERIALS, FROM STEEL I BEAMS TO WOODEN CHAIR RUNGS, ARE SUBJECT TO DESTRUCTIVE PHYSICAL FORCES.

**COMPRESSION**
PUSHED TOGETHER

**TENSION**
PULLED APART

**SHEAR**
CUT IN TWO

A FORCE IS SAID TO BE THAT WHICH TENDS TO CHANGE THE STATE OF REST OR MOTION OF A BODY. FORCES CANNOT BE SEEN. WE SEE ONLY WHAT THEY DO. THERE ARE TWO IMPORTANT CHARACTERISTICS THAT WE MUST KNOW ABOUT A FORCE, ITS MAGNITUDE AND DIRECTION, OR HOW BIG IT IS AND WHERE IT IS APPLIED. AN ARROW MAKES AN IDEAL SYMBOL FOR A FORCE. THE HEAD OF THE ARROW POINTS IN THE DIRECTION OF THE FORCE AND INDICATES WHERE IT IS APPLIED. THE SIZE OR LENGTH OF THE ARROW INDICATES THE MAGNITUDE OF THE FORCE.

WHEN A STRONG WIND PUSHES AGAINST THE SIDE OF A TALL BUILDING OR WHEN A CAT JUMPS ONTO A CHAIR, THE FORCES MAY BE THE SAME, ALTHOUGH OF CONSIDERABLE DIFFERENCE IN MAGNITUDE.

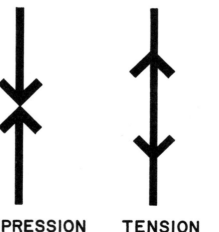

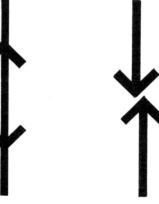

**COMPRESSION**   **TENSION**   **SHEAR**

# FORCE ARROW

*DIRECTION*

MAGNITUDE

THE PURPOSE OF DESCRIBING FORCES IS TO SHOW HOW THEY ACT ON A MATERIAL AND HOW THE MATERIAL REACTS TO STRESS. THE ABILITY OF THE MATERIAL TO RESIST THE THREE FORCES IS A MEASURE OF ITS UNIQUE QUALITIES AND SETS THE LIMITS OF ITS STRUCTURAL USE.

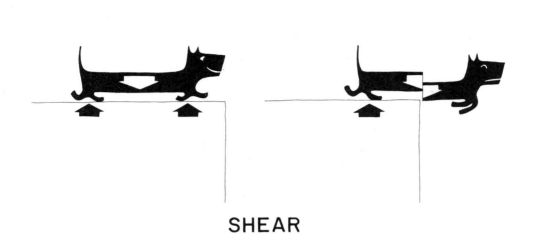

**SHEAR**

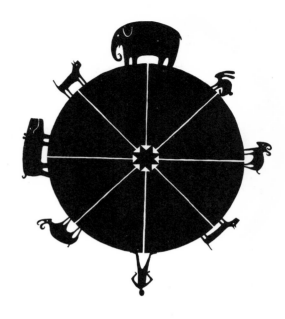

THE ONE CONSISTENT FORCE THAT ACTS CONTINUOUSLY
UPON ALL OBJECTS ON THE EARTH'S SURFACE IS THE
FORCE OF GRAVITY.  IT PULLS ALL THINGS IN A
STRAIGHT LINE TOWARD THE EARTH'S CENTER.

**COMPRESSION**

**TENSION**

# COMPARISON OF CHARACTERISTICS

# MATERIALS

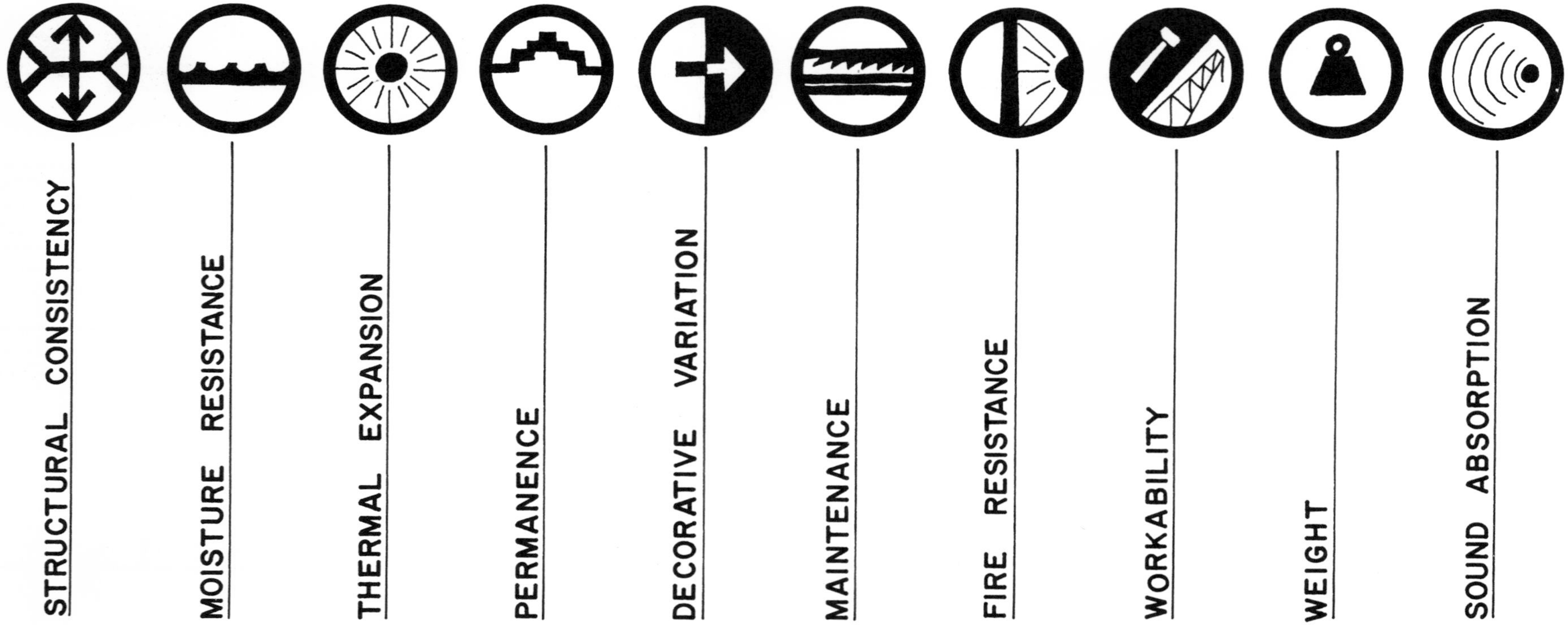

STRUCTURAL CONSISTENCY

MOISTURE RESISTANCE

THERMAL EXPANSION

PERMANENCE

DECORATIVE VARIATION

MAINTENANCE

FIRE RESISTANCE

WORKABILITY

WEIGHT

SOUND ABSORPTION

THE SELECTION OF A MATERIAL DEPENDS ON THE PARTICULAR DESIGN PROBLEM UNDER CONSIDERATION. A CHART LISTING MATERIALS AND CHARACTERISTICS IS A GRAPHIC METHOD OF VISUALIZING THE RANGE OF CHOICE.

BUILDING MATERIALS ARE SELECTED AFTER COMPARING CHARACTERISTICS. ALL MATERIALS ARE NOT LISTED HERE NOR ALL CHARACTERISTICS. THIS IS A SIMPLE METHOD FOR MAKING COMPARISONS, WHICH WE WILL USE THROUGHOUT THIS SECTION.

CONSISTENCY IS THE MATERIAL UNIFORM, HOMOGENEOUS, ISOTROPIC OR INCONSISTENT, VARIED, AND NONHOMOGENEOUS? HOW DOES IT REACT TO:

TENSION — COMPRESSION — SHEAR?

 MOISTURE RESISTANCE HOW STABLE DIMENSIONALLY IS THE MATERIAL WHEN WET OR DRY? WILL IT BE DESTROYED BY DAMPNESS?

 THERMAL EXPANSION HOW DO DIMENSIONS CHANGE WHEN THE MATERIAL ABSORBS HEAT?

 PERMANENCE WILL IT FADE IN SUNLIGHT OR DISINTEGRATE WITH AGE?

 DECORATIVE VARIATION HOW WIDE A RANGE OF TEXTURE AND COLOR IS POSSIBLE?

 MAINTENANCE HOW RESISTANT TO WEAR IS IT? HOW EASY TO MAINTAIN?

 FIRE RESISTANCE IS IT HIGHLY FLAMMABLE? IF IT BURNS, WILL IT EMIT DANGEROUS FUMES?

 WORKABILITY CAN IT BE WORKED EASILY WITH HAND TOOLS OR MUST IT BE FORMED AND SHAPED IN A FACTORY? HOW EASY IS IT TO INSTALL?

 WEIGHT HOW HEAVY IS THE MATERIAL? CAN IT BE LIFTED BY HAND OR ARE CRANES NECESSARY?

 SOUND ABSORPTION WILL IT KILL UNWANTED SOUND OR WILL IT REFLECT AND AMPLIFY NOISE? WILL IT DAMPEN WANTED SOUND?

NO MATERIAL HAS ALL OF THE IDEAL CHARACTERISTICS THAT THE DESIGNER DESIRES FOR EACH PARTICULAR DESIGN. A SELECTION IS MADE, THEREFORE, AFTER COMPARING CHARACTERISTICS.

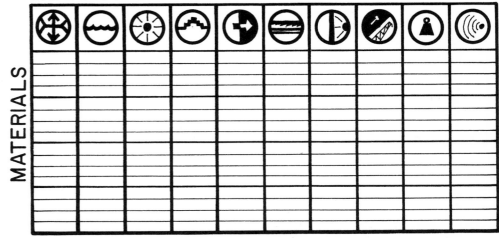

CHARACTERISTICS

MATERIALS

IT MUST ALSO BE REMEMBERED THAT MATERIALS ACT AND LOOK DIFFERENT WHEN USED IN THE THREE FORMS OF STRUCTURE. FOR EXAMPLE, WOOD USED AS LUMBER IS LINEAR, AS PLYWOOD IS PLANAR, AND AS A LOG CABIN IS SOLID.

LINE

PLANE

SOLID

# WOOD

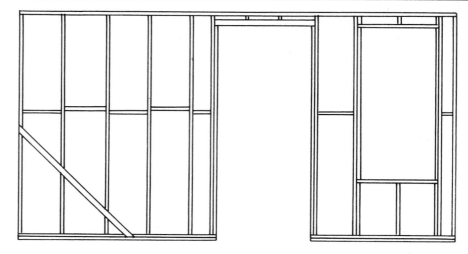

TREES ARE SUBJECT TO THE NATURAL ELEMENTS, WIND, SOIL, SUN, AND RAIN. WOOD IS THEREFORE RICH AND VARIED IN DECORATIVE QUALITIES BUT INCONSISTENT AS A BUILDING MATERIAL. THERE ARE KNOTS, PITCH POCKETS, CHECKS, AND SPLITS. INSECTS WILL EAT IT AND FUNGI DESTROY IT. MOISTURE MUST BE REMOVED, AND AS A RESULT WOOD SHRINKS AS IT DRIES AND SWELLS AGAIN WHEN IT ABSORBS MOISTURE WHICH CAUSES IT TO CURL, WARP, AND TWIST.

SOME WOODS ARE SOFT AND SOME HARD. NO TWO PIECES OF WOOD, EVEN FROM THE SAME TREE, ARE EXACTLY ALIKE.

ITS VIRTUES ARE WORKABILITY, WARMTH, AND BEAUTY.

SOFTWOODS ARE USED FOR STRUCTURE. THEY ARE CALLED CONIFERS OR CONIFEROUS BECAUSE MOST SPECIES BEAR CONES, HAVE NEEDLE-LIKE LEAVES, AND ARE GREEN ALL YEAR. THIS IS WHY THEY ARE CALLED EVERGREENS. FIR, PINE, SPRUCE, HEMLOCK AND REDWOOD ARE COMMON SOFTWOODS.

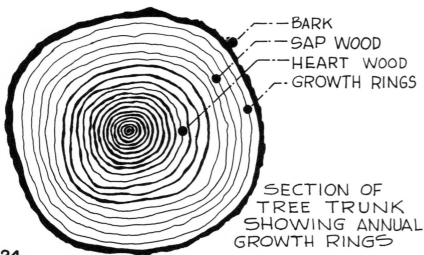

- BARK
- SAP WOOD
- HEART WOOD
- GROWTH RINGS

### SECTION OF TREE TRUNK SHOWING ANNUAL GROWTH RINGS

HARDWOODS ARE USED FOR INTERIOR PANELING, CABINETS, AND FURNITURE. THESE ARE BROADLEAVED TREES AND ARE CALLED DECIDUOUS BECAUSE THEY SHED THEIR LEAVES AT THE END OF EACH GROWTH SEASON. OAK, MAPLE, WALNUT, CHERRY, MAHOGANY, AND EBONY ARE COMMON HARDWOODS.

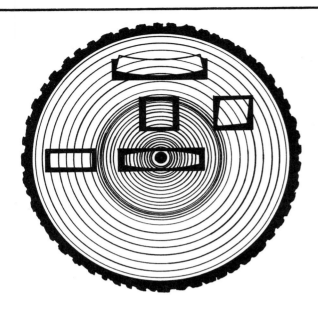

CHARACTERISTIC SHRINKAGE AND DISTORTION OF WOOD
MEMBERS IS CAUSED BY THE ANNUAL GROWTH RINGS WHEN
THE TREE IS CUT, SAWN INTO LUMBER, AND DRIED.

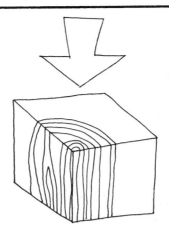

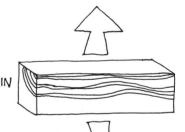

A COMPRESSIVE LOAD THAT CAN BE SUPPORTED
WITH THE GRAIN MAY CRUSH THE FIBERS
APPLIED ACROSS THE GRAIN

WEAK IN TENSION
ACROSS THE GRAIN

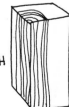

STRONG IN
TENSION WITH
THE GRAIN

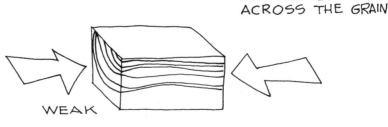

WEAK

STRONG

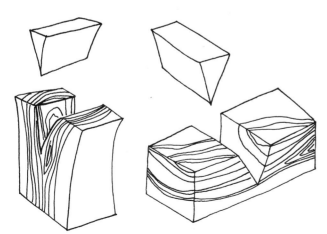

WOOD IS EASILY SPLIT IN THE GRAIN
DIRECTION BUT MUST BE CUT
ACROSS THE GRAIN

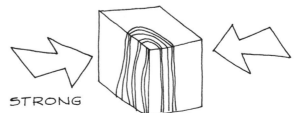

WOOD IS WEAK IN SHEAR IN
THE GRAIN DIRECTION

# WOOD-JOINTS

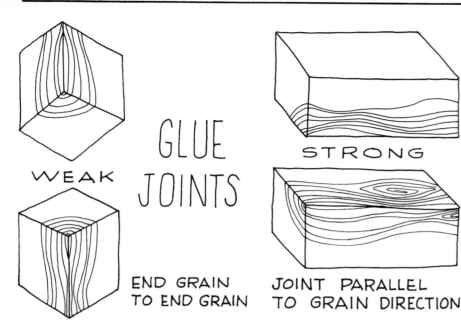

WEAK

END GRAIN
TO END GRAIN

GLUE
JOINTS

STRONG

JOINT PARALLEL
TO GRAIN DIRECTION

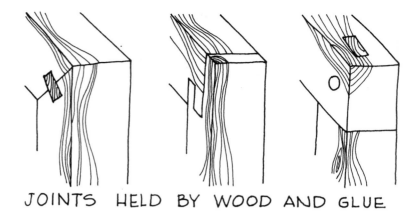

JOINTS HELD BY WOOD AND GLUE

JOINTS ARE OFTEN ATTRACTIVE DESIGN FEATURES BUT
THIS IS NOT THEIR MAIN PURPOSE. THE REASON FOR
A JOINT IS TO FASTEN TWO PIECES OF MATERIAL
TOGETHER.

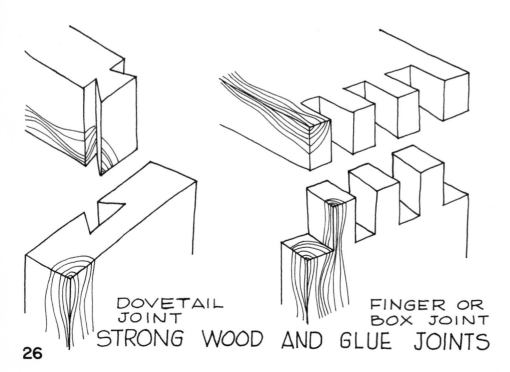

DOVETAIL
JOINT

FINGER OR
BOX JOINT

STRONG WOOD AND GLUE JOINTS

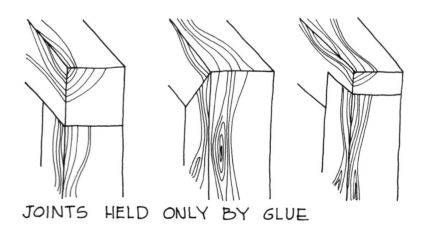

JOINTS HELD ONLY BY GLUE

MODERN MASTICS HAVE TREMENDOUS HOLDING POWER.
TRADITIONAL WOOD JOINTS WERE DESIGNED TO DEPEND
PRIMARILY ON THE STRENGTH OF THE WOOD.

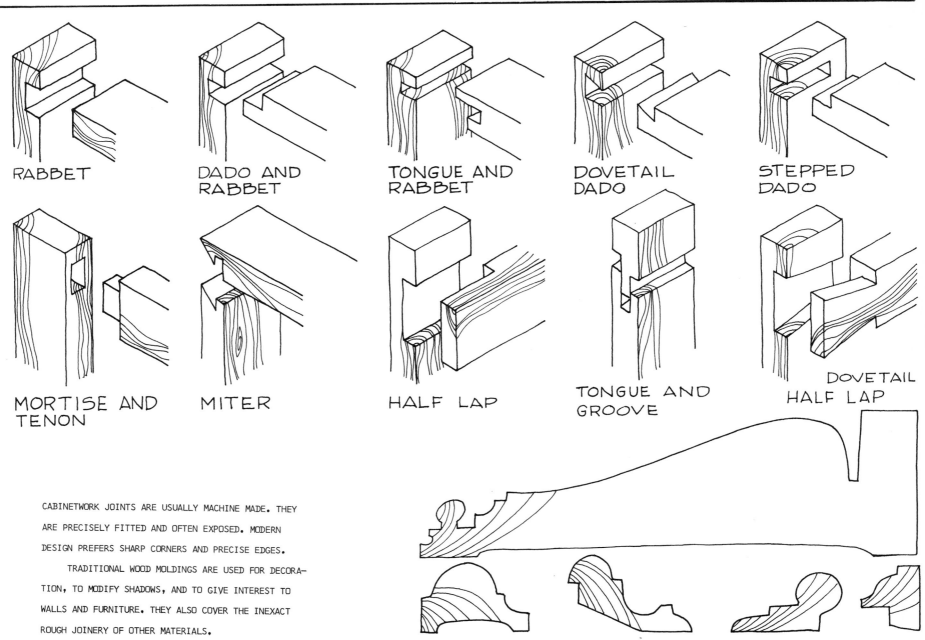

RABBET

DADO AND RABBET

TONGUE AND RABBET

DOVETAIL DADO

STEPPED DADO

MORTISE AND TENON

MITER

HALF LAP

TONGUE AND GROOVE

DOVETAIL HALF LAP

CABINETWORK JOINTS ARE USUALLY MACHINE MADE. THEY ARE PRECISELY FITTED AND OFTEN EXPOSED. MODERN DESIGN PREFERS SHARP CORNERS AND PRECISE EDGES.

TRADITIONAL WOOD MOLDINGS ARE USED FOR DECORATION, TO MODIFY SHADOWS, AND TO GIVE INTEREST TO WALLS AND FURNITURE. THEY ALSO COVER THE INEXACT ROUGH JOINERY OF OTHER MATERIALS.

MISCELLANEOUS MILLWORK     MOLDINGS

# WOOD FRAMING

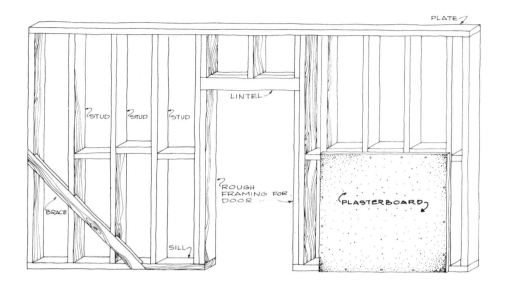

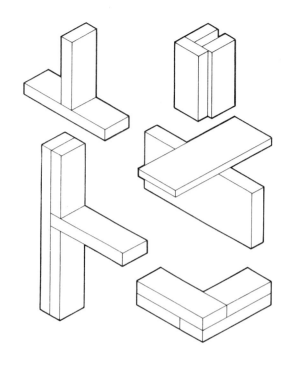

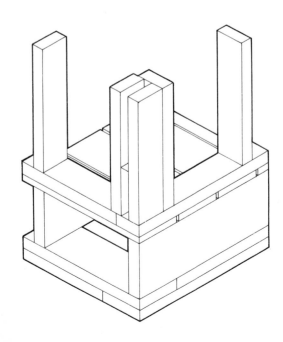

THE PRINCIPLES OF WOOD FRAMING ARE FAIRLY SIMPLE. THE INTERIOR DESIGNER USES FRAMING LUMBER TO MAKE PARTITIONS, ENCLOSURES, OR OTHER LIGHT NON-LOAD-BEARING CONSTRUCTIONS.

LIGHT WOOD MEMBERS ARE USED TO FORM A SKELETAL FRAMEWORK TO WHICH OTHER MATERIAL IS ATTACHED. WOOD IS FASTENED WITH NAILS, SCREWS, OR STAPLES. JOINTS ARE ROUGH AND COVERED OVER WITH OTHER MATERIALS. THE SIZE OF THE STRUCTURAL MEMBER DEPENDS ON THE SPANNING DIMENSION. MOST WALL PARTITIONS ARE MADE WITH 2 X 4'S. WHEN OPENINGS ARE CUT IN THE PARTITION, THE STUDS ARE DOUBLED AND THE SPANNING MEMBER IS INCREASED IN DEPTH. AT CORNERS THREE 2 X 4'S ARE USED TO PROVIDE A NAILING SURFACE FOR THE MATERIALS ON THE INTERIOR CORNER.

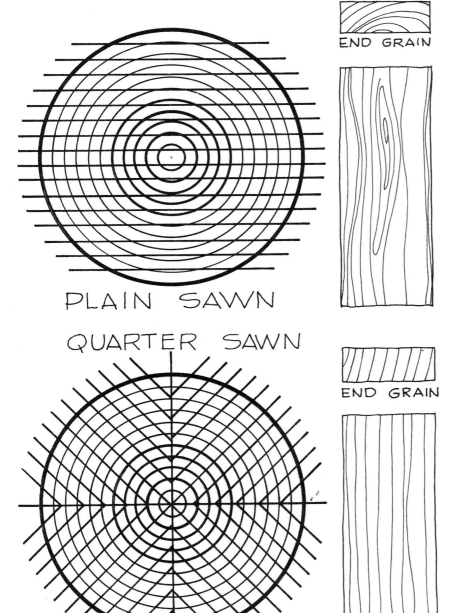

END GRAIN

PLAIN SAWN

QUARTER SAWN

END GRAIN

LUMBER CAN BE CUT FROM A LOG IN TWO DISTINCT WAYS: PLAINSAWED AND QUARTERSAWED. CUTTING TANGENT TO THE ANNUAL RINGS PRODUCES PLAINSAWED LUMBER IN SOFTWOODS, AND CUTTING RADIALLY TO THE RINGS OR PARALLEL TO THE RAYS PRODUCES QUARTERSAWED LUMBER IN HARDWOODS AND EDGE—GRAINED, OR VERTICAL—GRAINED LUMBER IN SOFTWOODS.

USUALLY SO—CALLED QUARTERSAWED OR EDGE—GRAINED LUMBER IS NOT CUT STRICTLY PARALLEL WITH THE RAYS, AND OFTEN IN PLAINSAWED BOARDS THE SURFACES NEXT TO THE EDGES ARE FAR FROM BEING TANGENT TO THE RINGS.

IN COMMERCIAL PRACTICE, LUMBER WITH RINGS AT ANGLES OF 45 DEGREES TO 90 DEGREES WITH THE SURFACE IS CALLED QUARTERSAWED, AND LUMBER WITH RINGS AT ANGLES OF 0 TO 45 DEGREES WITH THE SURFACE IS CALLED PLAINSAWED.

THE ADVANTAGE OF QUARTERSAWED LUMBER IS THAT IT SHRINKS AND SWELLS LESS AND DOES SO MORE UNIFORMLY. IT CHECKS AND SPLITS LESS IN DRYING AND IT WEARS MORE EVENLY. QUARTERSAWED WOOD IS MORE EXPENSIVE. IT IS SPECIFIED FOR WEARING SUR-FACES SUCH AS FLOORS.

THE CHARACTERISTICS OF WOOD USED AS LUMBER ARE LISTED IN THE CHART BELOW. THE CLOSER THE CHART COMES TO BEING TOTALLY BLACK THE CLOSER THE MATERIAL LISTED APPROACHES THE IDEAL CONDITION OF THE TEN LISTED CHARACTERISTICS, WHICH WERE DESCRIBED ON PAGE 23.

## CHARACTERISTICS

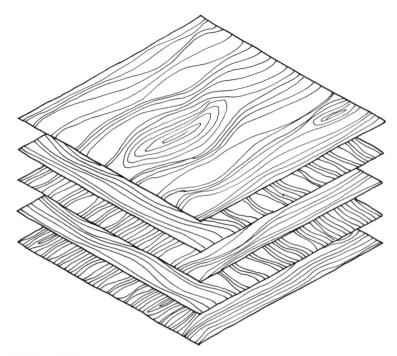

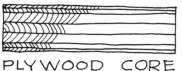

PLYWOOD CORE

3 PLY

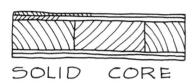

SOLID CORE

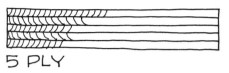

5 PLY

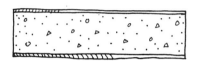

CHIP CORE

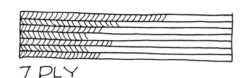

7 PLY

COMMON HARD-
WOOD FACED
PLYWOOD

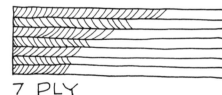

7 PLY

COMMON SOFT-
WOOD PLYWOOD

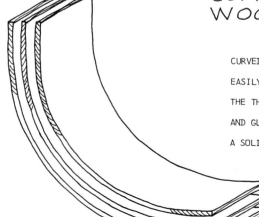

PLYWOOD REFERS TO LAMINATED WOODEN PANEL CONSTRUCTION OF SUCCESSIVE LAYERS OF THINLY CUT WOOD GLUED TOGETHER WITH THE GRAIN RUNNING IN OPPOSITE DIRECTIONS. THIS PROVIDES GREAT RESISTANCE TO CHECKING AND SPLITTING AND ADDED STRENGTH AND STABILITY.

PLYWOOD IS AN UNEVEN SANDWICH, THE NUMBER OF PLYS VARYING FROM 3 TO 9 OR MORE. PANELS ARE DESIGNATED BY THEIR INTERIOR CONSTRUCTION AS EITHER VENEER, LUMBER, OR CHIP CORE:

VENEER CORE THE ENTIRE PANEL IS COMPOSED OF THIN SANDWICH LAYERS OF WOOD.

LUMBER CORE THE FACE VENEER AND LAYER OF VENEER UNDERNEATH, CALLED THE CROSSBANDING, ARE THIN WOOD LAYERS. THE CENTER, OR CORE, IS MADE OF SOLID WOOD PIECES GLUED TOGETHER. THEY MAY BE A LITTLE OVER 1/2 INCH IN THICKNESS, DEPENDING ON THE THICKNESS OF THE ENTIRE PANEL.

CHIP CORE A CENTER OF BONDED WOOD CHIPS.

PLYWOOD COMES IN BOTH HARDWOOD AND SOFTWOOD. THE SOFTWOODS ARE USED MAINLY IN CONSTRUCTION AND THE HARDWOODS FOR FURNITURE AND DECORATIVE PANELING AND CABINETWORK.

CURVED PLYWOOD SECTIONS ARE EASILY MANUFACTURED BY BENDING THE THIN PLYS IN VARIOUS SHAPES AND GLUING THEM SEPARATELY INTO A SOLID PANEL.

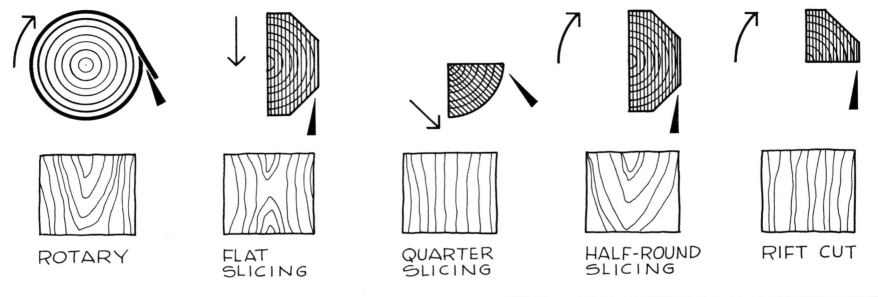

ROTARY  FLAT SLICING  QUARTER SLICING  HALF-ROUND SLICING  RIFT CUT

THE DECORATIVE GRAIN PATTERN OF PLYWOOD IS CAUSED BY THE WAY THE FACE VENEERS ARE SLICED FROM THE LOG. ROTARY CUTTING IS USUALLY USED FOR SOFTWOODS. DECORATIVE HARDWOODS ARE SLICED OR CUT.

BOOK MATCHED  SLIP MATCHED  RANDOM

VENEER MATCHING - TYPICAL MATCHING COMBINATIONS

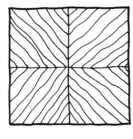

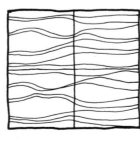

DIAMOND  REVERSE  END MATCHED

# PLYWOOD JOINTS

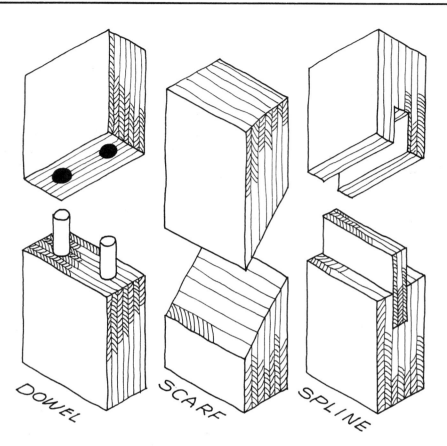

DOWEL     SCARF     SPLINE

## PLYWOOD PANEL JOINTS

THE PURPOSE OF A PLYWOOD PANEL STRUCTURAL JOINT IS TO PRESERVE THE
STRUCTURAL INTEGRITY OF THE TWO PIECES AS AN UNBROKEN SURFACE.

PLYWOOD IS A LARGE SHEET MATERIAL. IT WILL COVER LARGE AREAS,
AND ITS LAMINATED CONSTRUCTION GIVES IT STRENGTH IN ALL DIR-
ECTIONS. IT IS LIGHT, STRONG, AND EASY TO WORK.

PLYWOOD WILL DEFLECT MORE
THAN SOLID WOOD BECAUSE OF
THE CROSS GRAIN RUNNING IN
THE SHORT DIRECTION.

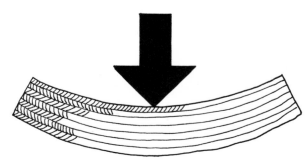

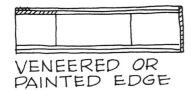

VENEERED OR
PAINTED EDGE

HARDWOOD
EDGE

MITERED
HARDWOOD
EDGE

CONCEALED
HARDWOOD
EDGE

PLASTIC
LAMINATE EDGE
TOP AND BOTTOM

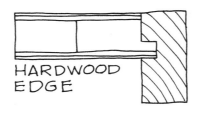

HARDWOOD
EDGE

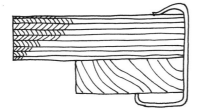

CLIP ON METAL
EDGE

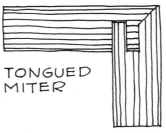

RAISED
HARDWOOD
EDGE

## PANEL EDGES

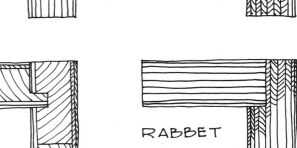

TONGUED
MITER

SPLINED
MITER

DADO

RABBET

## CORNER DETAILS

PLYWOOD IS DETAILED THE SAME AS OTHER WOODS IN
CABINETWORK EXCEPT FOR THE EDGES. TO KEEP FROM
EXPOSING THE LESS ATTRACTIVE CORE, A VARIETY OF
EDGING DETAILS ARE USED.

## CHARACTERISTICS

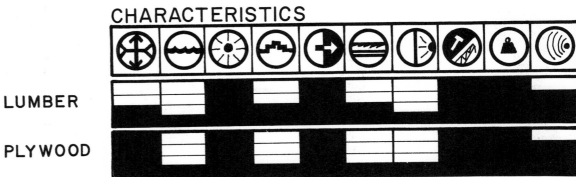

LUMBER

PLYWOOD

# MASONRY

ALTHOUGH MASONRY IS DEFINED AS THAT WORK DONE BY MASONS, WHICH INCLUDES BRICK, TILE, CONCRETE AND GYPSUM BLOCK, FLUE LININGS, AND STONEWORK, THE INTERIOR DESIGNER IS USUALLY ONLY CONCERNED WITH WHAT WE WILL DEFINE AS MODULAR, MAN-MADE BUILDING ELEMENTS.

THERE ARE ESSENTIALLY THREE KINDS OF MASONRY IN THIS CATEGORY: UNITS HARDENED BY HEAT LIKE CLAY PRODUCTS, UNITS HARDENED BY CHEMICAL ACTION LIKE CONCRETE AND GYPSUM BLOCK, AND UNITS NATURALLY HARDENED, LIKE STONE, WHICH ARE CUT AND TRUED TO MAKE THEM USABLE.

THE INTERIOR DESIGNER IS SELDOM CONCERNED WITH THE LOAD-BEARING CAPACITIES OF MASONRY WALLS OTHER THAN THEIR ABILITY TO SUPPORT THEIR OWN WEIGHT. APPEARANCE, COLOR, AND TEXTURE ARE IMPORTANT, BUT PERHAPS THE MOST IMPORTANT FEATURE OF MASONRY IS THE SCALE IT IMPARTS TO THE INTERIOR. A BRICK IS SCALED TO A MASON'S HAND AND THEREFORE CONFORMS WELL TO THE DIMENSIONS OF THE HUMAN BODY. A CONCRETE BLOCK IS DESIGNED TO FACILITATE THE ERECTION OF WALLS QUICKLY AND ECONOMICALLY. IT MUST BE SET WITH TWO HANDS. THE AWKWARDNESS OF INSTALLATION IS REFLECTED IN ITS SCALE, WHICH IS OVERSIZED FOR MOST INTERIORS.

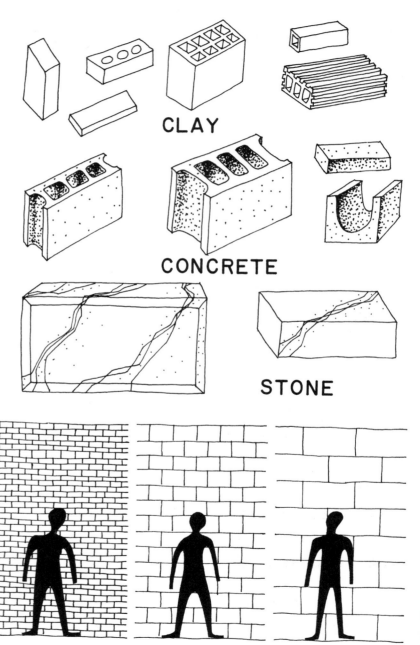

CLAY

CONCRETE

STONE

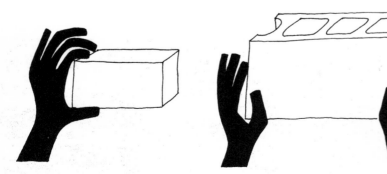

STRENGTH GEOMETRY

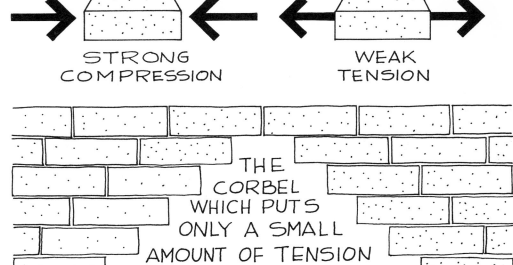

STRONG COMPRESSION

WEAK TENSION

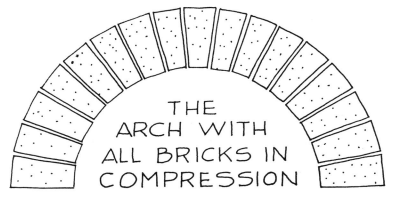

THE ARCH WITH ALL BRICKS IN COMPRESSION

THE CORBEL WHICH PUTS ONLY A SMALL AMOUNT OF TENSION STRESS ON EACH BRICK

A SIMPLE PRINCIPLE DETERMINES THE TRADITIONAL BRICK BONDING PATTERNS. BRICKS ARE STRONGER THAN THE MORTAR THAT BONDS THEM. THE STRENGTH OF A WALL DEPENDS ON ITS ABILITY TO ACT AS AN INTEGRAL UNIT, THAT IS, ONE HOMOGENEOUS MASS WITHOUT PLANES OF WEAKNESS.

BRICKS ARE BONDED, OR LAID, IN SUCH A WAY THAT THEY CROSS OVER THE WEAK MORTAR JOINTS SO THAT THE WALL HAS NO CONTINUOUS MORTAR JOINTS IN VERTICAL SECTION. HORIZONTAL JOINTS ARE CONTINUOUS BECAUSE THE WEIGHT OF THE MASONRY STRUCTURE AFFORDS STABILITY IN THIS DIMENSION.

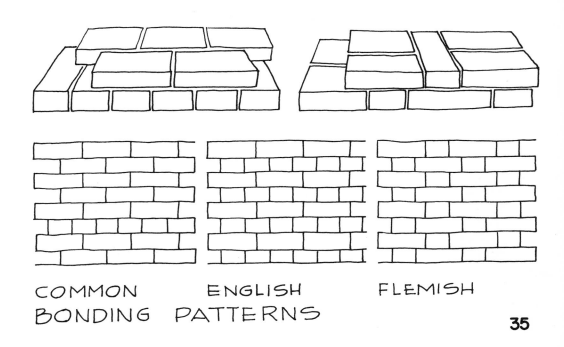

COMMON        ENGLISH        FLEMISH

BONDING   PATTERNS

# BRICK MODULE

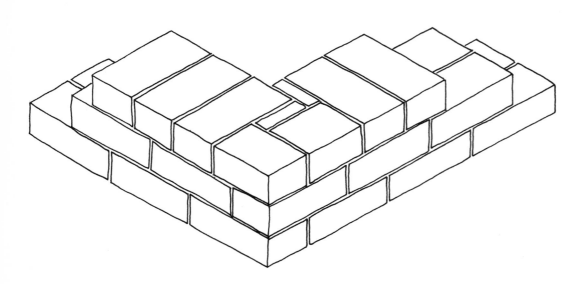

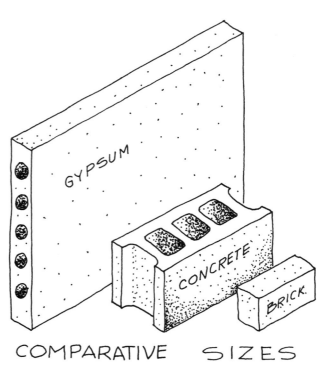

COMPARATIVE SIZES

THE MODULE IN ARCHITECTURE REFERS TO A STANDARD UNIT OF MEASUREMENT. THE
BRICK IS A GOOD DEMONSTRATION OF THIS PRINCIPLE. THE WIDTH IS ONE-HALF OF
THE LENGTH. WHEN LAID CROSSWISE IN A WALL, IT ALIGNS WITH BOTH THE EXTERIOR
AND INTERIOR SURFACES. WHEN WALLS ARE THICKENED BEYOND ONE INCH LENGTH,
BRICKS CAN BE ARRANGED TO BREAK THE JOINT AND STILL ALIGN BECAUSE OF THEIR
MODULAR DIMENSIONS. WHEN THE MODULAR DIMENSION OF THE WALL IS CHANGED, SUCH
AS TURNING A CORNER, ODD SIZES SUCH AS QUARTER, HALF, AND THREE-QUARTER
BRICKS ARE USED TO FILL OUT THE WALL.

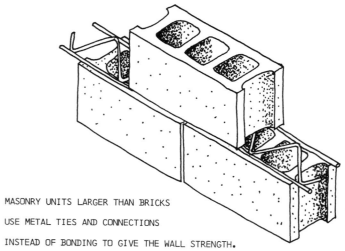

MASONRY UNITS LARGER THAN BRICKS
USE METAL TIES AND CONNECTIONS
INSTEAD OF BONDING TO GIVE THE WALL STRENGTH.

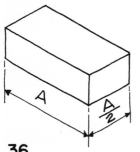

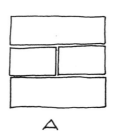

A

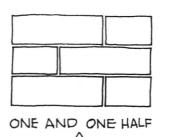

ONE AND ONE HALF
A

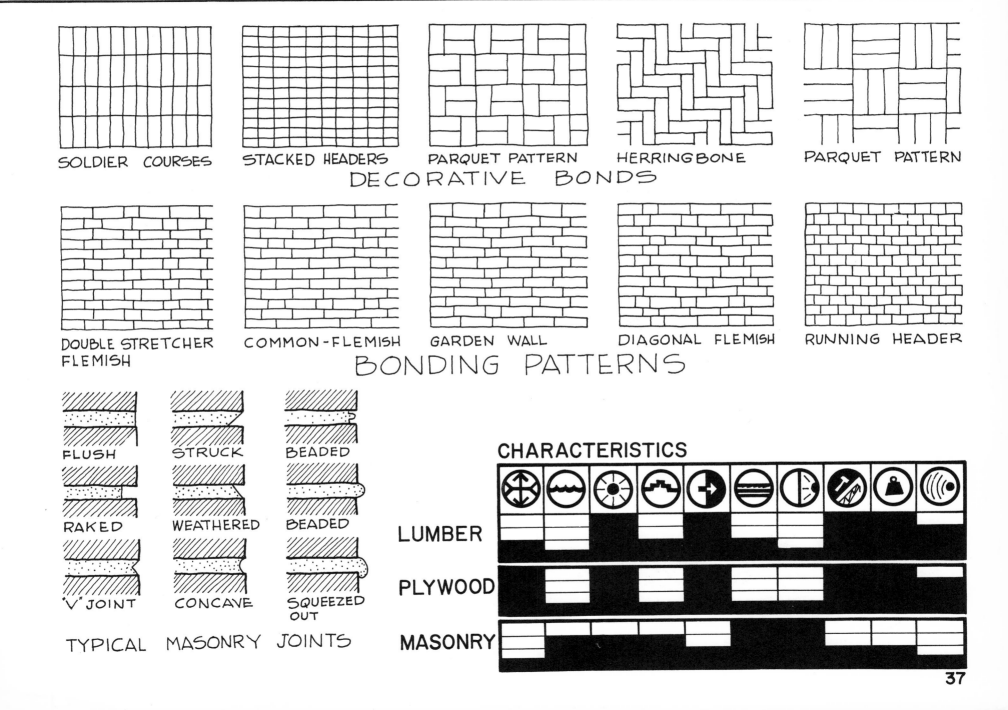

SOLDIER COURSES    STACKED HEADERS    PARQUET PATTERN    HERRINGBONE    PARQUET PATTERN

## DECORATIVE BONDS

DOUBLE STRETCHER FLEMISH    COMMON-FLEMISH    GARDEN WALL    DIAGONAL FLEMISH    RUNNING HEADER

## BONDING PATTERNS

FLUSH    STRUCK    BEADED

RAKED    WEATHERED    BEADED

'V' JOINT    CONCAVE    SQUEEZED OUT

## TYPICAL MASONRY JOINTS

## CHARACTERISTICS

LUMBER

PLYWOOD

MASONRY

# METAL

IRON AND STEEL ARE COMMONLY USED IN THE STRUCTURAL FRAMES OF BUILDINGS. ALTHOUGH THE INTERIOR DESIGNER IS PRIMARILY INVOLVED WITH LIGHT-GAUGE STEEL MEMBERS IN THE CONSTRUCTION OF FURNITURE, DOOR, AND WINDOW FRAMES, IT IS OCCASIONALLY NECESSARY TO USE HEAVIER STEEL ROLLED SECTIONS.

STRUCTURAL STEEL FABRICATION TAKES PLACE IN A FABRICATING SHOP, AND STEEL PIECES ARE BROUGHT TO THE SITE READY TO ASSEMBLE. THE MATERIAL IS HEAVY, CANNOT EASILY BE WORKED ON THE JOB, AND REQUIRES SPECIAL EQUIPMENT FOR PLACING.

THE STEEL FRAME OF A BUILDING IS A SKELETAL CAGE WHICH IS FILLED IN WITH OTHER MATERIALS.

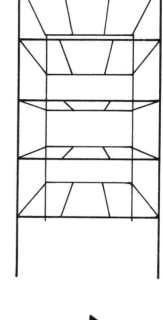

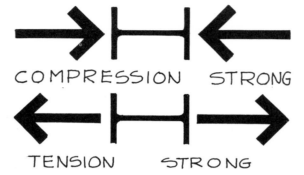

COMPRESSION   STRONG

TENSION   STRONG

STRUCTURAL STEEL SECTIONS

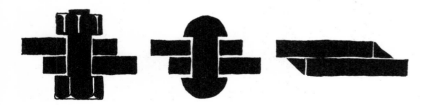

BOLT     RIVET     WELD

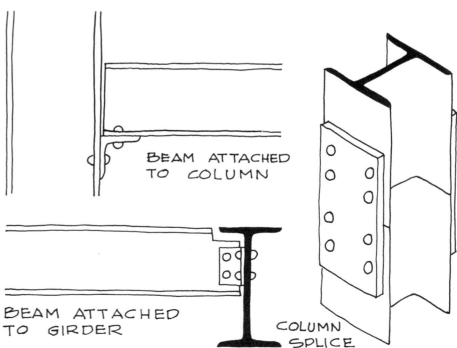

BEAM ATTACHED TO COLUMN

BEAM ATTACHED TO GIRDER

COLUMN SPLICE

SEAMLESS TUBING

CHANNELS AND ANGLES

ZEE'S AND TEE'S

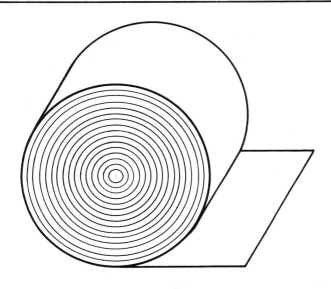

LIGHT-GAUGE STEEL SHAPES MADE OF ROLLED STEEL ARE MORE COMMONLY USED BY THE INTERIOR DE-SIGNER THAN STRUCTURAL STEEL SECTIONS.

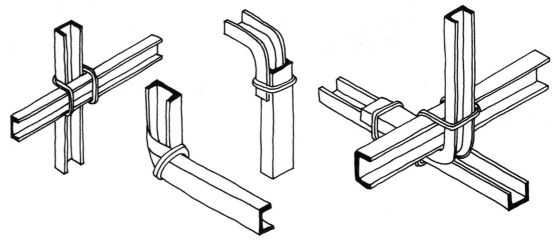

METAL CHANNELS ARE BENT AND TIED WITH WIRE FOR METAL FRAMING FOR LATH AND PLASTER

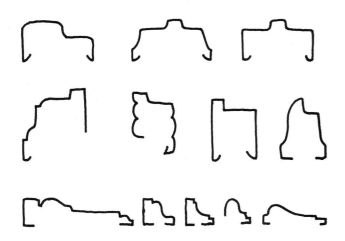

SHEET STEEL IS BENT TO A VARIETY OF SHAPES TO MAKE DOOR BUCKS AND METAL MOLDINGS. METAL MOLDINGS CAN BE FOUND IN ALMOST ALL THE SHAPES IN WHICH TRADITIONAL WOOD MOLDINGS ARE MANUFACTURED.

SHEET STEEL IS OFTEN PREFINISHED WITH PAINT, LACQUER, OR VINYL FINISH BEFORE IT IS FABRICATED. PREFINISHED STEEL MUST BE JOINED WITHOUT USING HEAT, WHICH WOULD DESTROY ITS FINISH.

# EXTRUDED METAL SHAPES

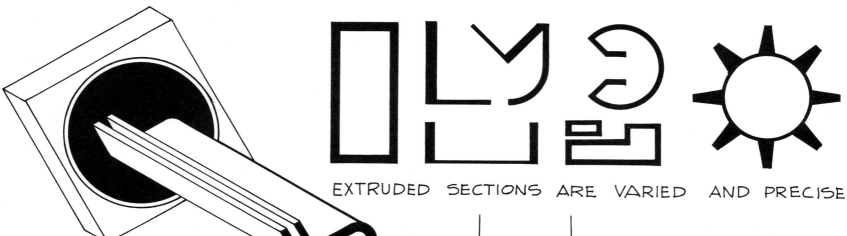

## EXTRUDED METAL SECTION

EXTRUSION DIES ARE EXPENSIVE, BUT IF A LOT OF MATERIAL IS TO
BE USED THEY CAN BE QUITE ECONOMICAL. THE DESIGNER CAN DESIGN
THE DIE SHAPE DESIRED.

EXTRUDED SECTIONS ARE VARIED AND PRECISE

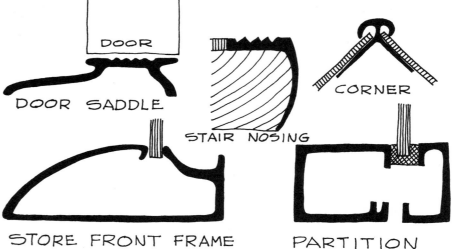

DOOR SADDLE

STAIR NOSING

CORNER

STORE FRONT FRAME

PARTITION

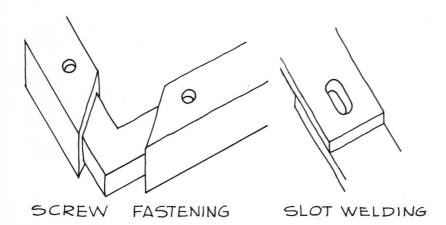

SCREW FASTENING

SLOT WELDING

JOINING NONFERROUS METALS FOR THE INTERIOR MUST BE PRECISE.
SCREWING, BOLTING, OR SPOT OR SLOT WELDING IS USED.

THE ARCHITECTURAL NONFERROUS METALS ARE COPPER, BRONZE (AN ALLOY
OF COPPER AND OTHER METALS) AND ALUMINUM. ALUMINUM IS THE MOST
COMMONLY USED. NONFERROUS METALS ARE SOFTER THAN IRON OR STEEL
AND CAN BE EXTRUDED AND WORKED MUCH MORE EASILY. ALUMINUM CAN BE
CUT AND FILED WITH WOODWORKING TOOLS. IT IS DIFFICULT TO WELD SO
IT IS USUALLY FASTENED WITH SCREWS AND SPECIAL FASTENINGS. NON-
FERROUS METALS ARE SELDOM USED EXCEPT FOR DECORATION.

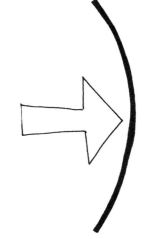

BENT FOR RIGIDITY

BUILT UP THIN METAL SHEETS FOR STRENGTH AND RIGIDITY

RESISTS WEAR—BUT FINISHES USUALLY DAMAGE EASILY

ALMOST UNLIMITED FORMAL POSSIBILITY

STRONG—BUT DIFFICULT TO CUT AND FIT

THIN METAL SHEETS BEND EASILY

WILL ONLY BURN AT HIGH TEMPERATURES BUT WILL LOSE ITS STRENGTH AT COMPARATIVELY LOW HEAT—FIREPROOFED

MUST BE PAINTED TO PROTECT FROM RUST

## CHARACTERISTICS

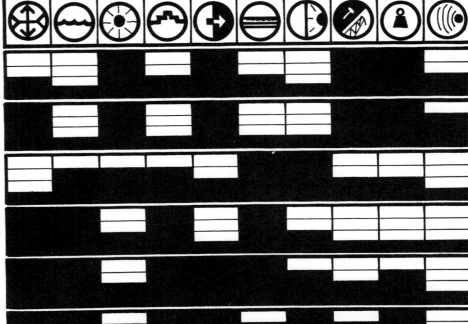

LUMBER

PLYWOOD

MASONRY

STRUCTURAL STEEL

SHEET METAL

ALUMINUM

# LIQUID STONE

# CONCRETE

CEMENT AND WATER ACT AS A PASTE TO GLUE MATERIALS SUCH AS SAND AND COARSER MATERIALS SUCH AS BROKEN STONE, GRAVEL, BLAST FURNACE SLAG, OR CINDERS TOGETHER. WHEN THE MASS HARDENS, IT BECOMES STONELIKE.

CONCRETE HAS GREAT COMPRESSIVE STRENGTH BUT VERY LITTLE ABILITY TO RESIST TENSION. STEEL BARS, RODS, OR STEEL MESH FABRIC ARE INCORPORATED IN THOSE PARTS OF CONCRETE MEMBERS WHERE TENSILE STRENGTH IS DESIRED. CONCRETE CAN THEREFORE BE DIVIDED INTO TWO CATEGORIES, REINFORCED AND MASS, OR UNREIN-FORCED, CONCRETE.

THE LIQUID MASS MUST BE RESTRAINED UNTIL IT IS HARDENED. ITS FORM DEPENDS ON THE MATERIALS USED TO KEEP IT IN PLACE. THESE ARE CALLED FORMS AND ARE MADE OF STEEL, WOOD, FIBERGLASS, AND SOMETIMES THE EARTH ITSELF.

THE INTERIOR DESIGNER IS USUALLY MOST INTERESTED IN THE SURFACE FINISH OF THE CONCRETE. PLAIN CEMENT IS GRAY BUT IT CAN ALSO BE HAD IN WHITE AND BROWN.

COLORS CAN BE ADDED TO THE CEMENT BUT CONCRETE USUALLY TAKES ITS COLOR FROM THE AGGREGATES USED IN THE MIXTURE. THESE COMPOSE THE MAJOR VOLUME OF THE MIXTURE AND THEREFORE GIVE THE CONCRETE ITS DISTINCTIVE COLOR AND TEXTURE.

CONCRETE IS VERY HEAVY, LIKE STONE, AND WILL WEATHER LIKE STONE. CONCRETE IS USED IN INTERIOR DESIGN AS PART OF THE EXPOSED STRUCTURE OF THE BUILDING OR LIKE STONE IN DECORATIVE PANELS. IT IS SELDOM A MAJOR MATERIAL IN INTERIORS BECAUSE OF ITS WEIGHT.

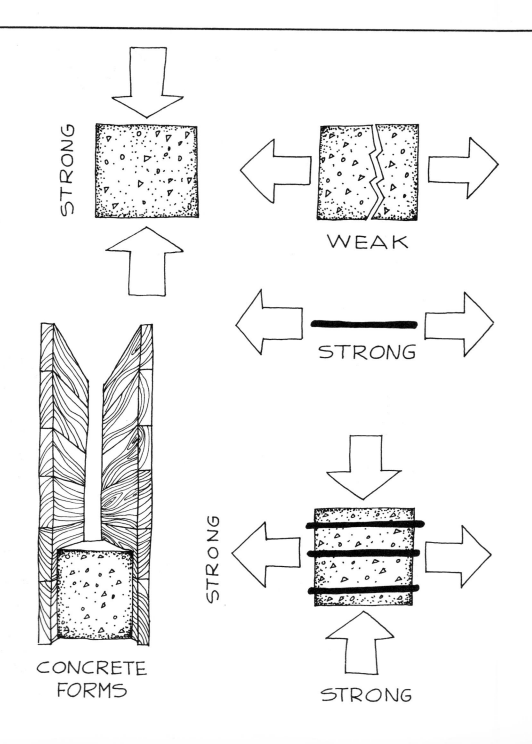

STRONG

WEAK

STRONG

CONCRETE FORMS

STRONG

STRONG

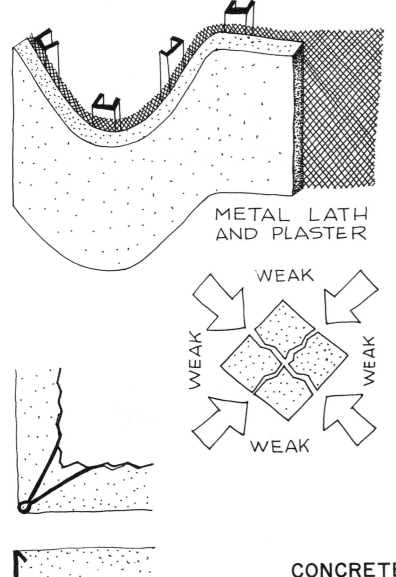

METAL LATH
AND PLASTER

PLASTER IS APPLIED AS A FINISH TO WALLS AND CEILINGS IN THE
INTERIOR OF BUILDINGS. IT CAN BE MOLDED AND TROWELED. ON SETTING,
IT FORMS A HARD SURFACE WHICH WILL HOLD PAINT OR WALLCOVERING.
IT INSULATES AGAINST THE PASSAGE OF HEAT, AIR, AND SOUND. IT CAN BE
USED TO CONTROL SOUND WITH SPECIAL SURFACE TEXTURES AND AGGREGATES.

PLASTER CAN BE APPLIED TO MASONRY, WOOD, OR METAL LATH. THE
VARIETY OF FORMS DEPENDS ALMOST ENTIRELY UPON THE SUPPORTING
MATERIAL. SHEETS OF PLASTER COVERED WITH PAPER, CALLED PLASTERBOARD,
ARE USED AS WALL AND CEILING SURFACES. PLASTER BLOCKS ARE SOMETIMES
USED TO MAKE WALLS.

WEAK WEAK WEAK WEAK WEAK

FLAT SHEETS

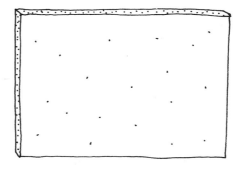

PLASTERBOARD

SOLID WALLS

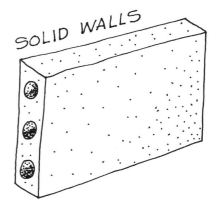

PLASTER BLOCK

METAL SHAPES
PROTECT CORNERS

CONCRETE
REINFORCED

PLASTER

## CHARACTERISTICS

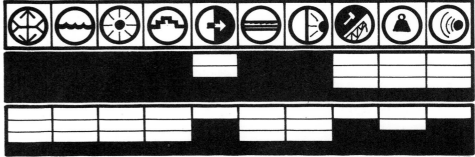

# WEIGHING  DECISIONS

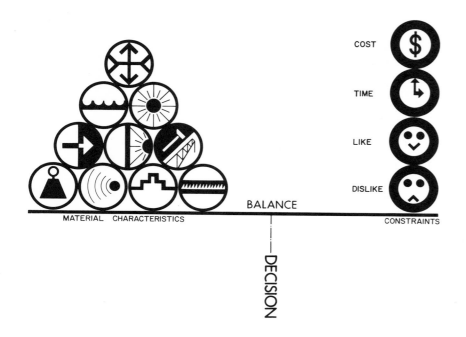

MATERIAL  CHARACTERISTICS

BALANCE

DECISION

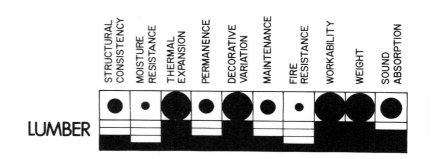

COST

TIME

LIKE

DISLIKE

CONSTRAINTS

| | STRUCTURAL CONSISTENCY | MOISTURE RESISTANCE | THERMAL EXPANSION | PERMANENCE | DECORATIVE VARIATION | MAINTENANCE | FIRE RESISTANCE | WORKABILITY | WEIGHT | SOUND ABSORPTION |
|---|---|---|---|---|---|---|---|---|---|---|
| LUMBER | ● | · | ● | ● | ● | · | · | ● | ● | ● |

THE MATERIAL CHARACTERISTICS ARE SHOWN AS
CIRCLES IN THIS LUMBER CHART.  A SMALL DOT
MEANS THAT THIS PARTICULAR ATTRIBUTE DOES
NOT WEIGH VERY HEAVILY IN THE MATERIAL'S
FAVOR.

DESIGN IS CHOICE.  AS MANY OF THE PROBLEM ELEMENTS AS POSSIBLE MUST
BE BROUGHT INTO CONSCIOUS CONSIDERATION IF THE DESIGNER IS TO ACHIEVE
A BALANCE.

THIS IS MERELY A GRAPHIC MEANS OF COMPARING CHOICE IN THE DIFFER-
ENCES OF MATERIALS; A GATHERING TOGETHER OF INFORMATION IN A VISUAL WAY
SO THAT THE DESIGNER CAN CONSIDER THE ALTERNATIVES OF CHOICE.

IT IS NOT SCIENTIFIC, NOR IS IT MEANT TO BE.  THE ULTIMATE DECISION
DEPENDS ON THE YES AND NO OF INTUITIVE CHOICE, THE UNIQUE PREFERENCE OF
EACH HUMAN BEING.

THIS IS A GRAPHIC PATTERN PRESENTING CHOICES TO INSPIRE THE DESIGNER'S
SELECTION.  THE BETTER THE PATTERN AND THE MORE ACCURATELY IT REFLECTS ALL
OF THE ELEMENTS OF THE PROBLEM, THE BETTER THE DESIGNER'S INTUITION CAN BE
BROUGHT INTO PLAY.

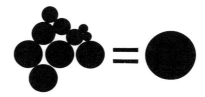

ALL ATTRIBUTES HAVE BEEN ADDED TOGETHER INTO
COMPARATIVE SPHERES.  THE SIZE OF THE SPHERES
WILL CHANGE IF SOME OF THE FACTORS DO NOT
HAVE TO BE CONSIDERED UNDER CERTAIN DESIGN
CONDITIONS.  FOR EXAMPLE IF MOISTURE AND
FIRE RESISTANCE DO NOT HAVE TO BE CONSIDERED,
LUMBER WEIGHS MORE HEAVILY UPON THE SCALE OF
ACCEPTANCE.

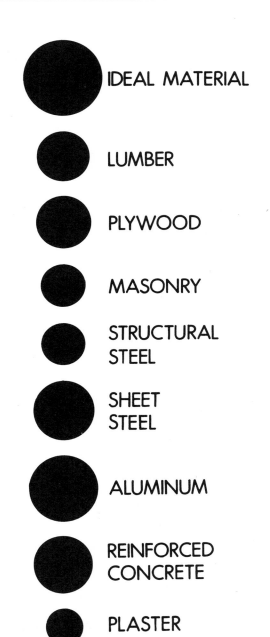

IDEAL MATERIAL

LUMBER

PLYWOOD

MASONRY

STRUCTURAL
STEEL

SHEET
STEEL

ALUMINUM

REINFORCED
CONCRETE

PLASTER

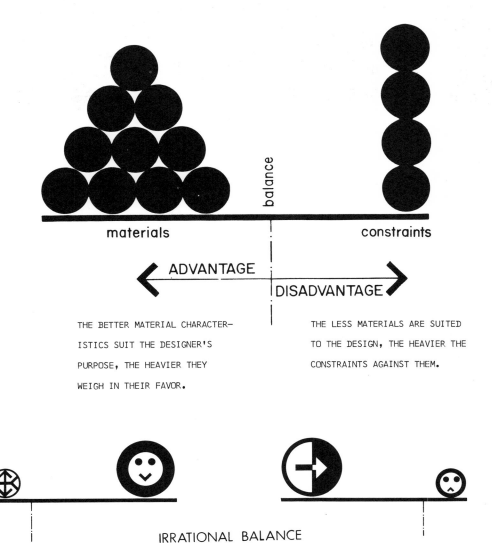

balance

materials                                                    constraints

← ADVANTAGE

DISADVANTAGE →

THE BETTER MATERIAL CHARACTER-                THE LESS MATERIALS ARE SUITED
ISTICS SUIT THE DESIGNER'S                    TO THE DESIGN, THE HEAVIER THE
PURPOSE, THE HEAVIER THEY                      CONSTRAINTS AGAINST THEM.
WEIGH IN THEIR FAVOR.

IRRATIONAL BALANCE

AS WE SAID IN THE INTRODUCTION, REASON ONLY GOES SO FAR.  PREFERENCES, LIKES,
AND DISLIKES OF MATERIALS MAY WEIGH FOR OR AGAINST THEM, BUT THIS IS A DECISION
THAT MUST BE MADE CONSCIOUSLY AFTER ALL OF THE MATERIALS' OTHER ATTRIBUTES HAVE
BEEN WEIGHED IN THE BALANCE.

PLASTICS ARE ALMOST THE IDEAL MATERIAL WE SAID DID NOT EXIST.  PLASTICS CAN BE DESIGNED FOR ALMOST ANY USE.  THEY CAN BE MADE RESISTANT TO WEAR AND THEIR COLORS CONTROLLED AT WILL.  A WIDE RANGE OF TEXTURES ARE ALSO POSSIBLE.  THE ONLY AREAS IN WHICH THEIR USE IS SOMETIMES QUESTIONED ARE FIRE RESISTANCE, ACTION IN SUNLIGHT, AGING, AND RESISTANCE TO RODENT ATTACK.

PLASTICS MAY BE SOFT, TOUGH, HARD, BRITTLE, MALLEABLE, TRANSPARENT, OPAQUE, EASILY COLORED, OR RESISTANT TO PIGMENTATION.  THEY MAY BURN READILY OR BE RESISTANT TO FIRE, DETERIORATE QUICKLY OR BE ALMOST IMPERVIOUS TO WEATHERING.

PLASTICS ARE SYNTHETIC MATERIALS, PRODUCTS OF THE CHEMICAL INDUSTRY, WHICH CONVERTS RAW MATERIALS INTO NEW AND RADICALLY DIFFERENT FORMS.  THEY CAN BE ALMOST ANYTHING THAT MAN WANTS THEM TO BE.

THERE ARE OVER 30 VARIETIES OF MATERIALS CALLED PLASTICS, AND MOST OF THEM CAN BE COMBINED WITH EACH OTHER.  THIRTY POSSIBLE COMBINATIONS ADD UP TO 2632528598 AND 21 ZEROS MORE.  ALL CANNOT BE COMBINED IN ALL WAYS BUT THE NUMBER OF POSSIBILITIES IS STILL STAGGERING.

PLASTICS ARE CALLED PLASTICS BECAUSE AT SOME STAGE THEY ARE PLASTIC, AS IS EVERY OTHER MATERIAL, INCLUDING STONE, WHICH IS PLASTIC AT THE TREMENDOUS TEMPERATURES BELOW THE EARTH'S SURFACE.

PLASTICS MAY BE PLASTIC ONLY ONCE IN THEIR USE OR MAY CONTINUALLY REVERT TO A PLASTIC STATE WHEN HEAT IS REAPPLIED.  THE THERMO-PLASTICS BECOME SOFTER AS TEMPERATURES RAISE AND HARDEN AS THEY FALL.  THE THERMOSET-PLASTICS ARE FORMED BY HEAT AND RESIST TEMPERATURE VARIATIONS MUCH BETTER, BUT EVEN SOME OF THESE WILL SOFTEN AND HARDEN NOTICEABLY WITH TEMPERATURE VARIATIONS.

PLASTICS ARE USED AS ADHESIVES, AS CORES OF SANDWICH PANELS, WINDOWS, SASH, FRAMES, HOUSE SHELLS, GLAZING, WEATHER STRIPPING, DOORS, FABRICS, CORRE-GATED SHEETS, HARDWARE, HANDRAILS, AND ALMOST ANYTHING ELSE ONE CAN NAME, WHICH ONE WOULD EXPECT OF SUCH A DIVERSE MATERIAL.  THESE ARE ONLY SOME OF ITS USES IN BUILDING, TO SAY NOTHING OF ITS APPLICATION IN PRODUCTS OF OTHER INDUSTRIES THAT MAY ALSO HAVE BUILDING USES.

HOW DO WE THINK ABOUT A MATERIAL WHICH IN REALITY HAS ALMOST ALL THE CHARACTERISTICS OF ALL OTHER MATERIALS ROLLED INTO ONE?  ONE SOLUTION IS TO JUDGE ITS POSSIBLE USE BY THE MEANS EMPLOYED TO SHAPE AND FORM IT.  THE WAY MATERIALS ARE FORMED CAN GIVE US SOME IDEA OF THE CONTROL WE CAN EXERT OVER THEM.

## CASTING

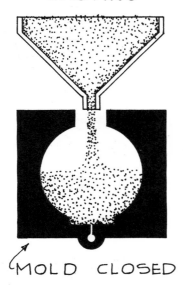

MOLD CLOSED

MOLD REMOVED

## EXTRUSION

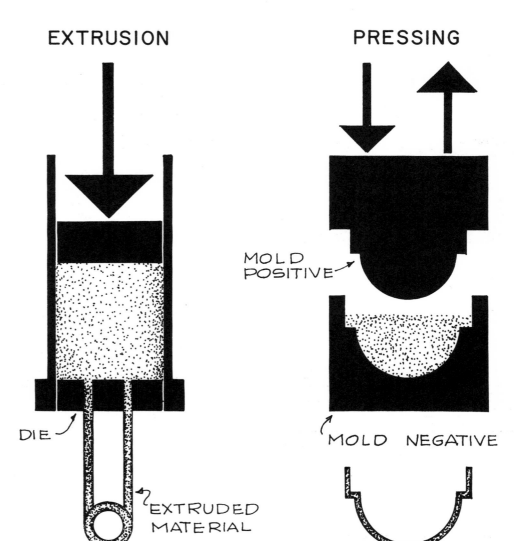

DIE

EXTRUDED MATERIAL

## PRESSING

MOLD POSITIVE

MOLD NEGATIVE

AMORPHOUS MATERIAL HELD IN A MOLD UNTIL IT HARDENS: PLASTER, CONCRETE, PLASTICS, CLAY, GLASS, AND METALS.

PLASTIC MATERIAL SQUEEZED THROUGH A FORMING DIE: PLASTICS, METALS, AND CLAY.

SHAPELESS MATERIAL FORMED BY PRESSURE IN MOLD: PLASTICS, CLAY, AND METAL.

# FORMING SHEET MATERIAL

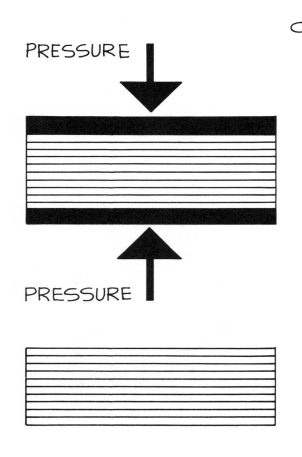

PRESSURE

PRESSURE

COMPOUND

ROLLED SHEET MATERIAL

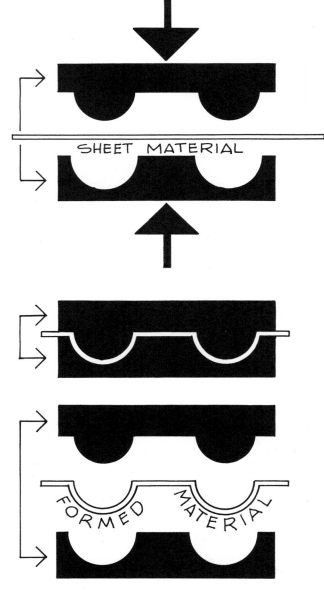

SHEET MATERIAL

FORMED MATERIAL

IN LAMINATING SHEET MATERIAL THIN LAYERS OF MATERIAL ARE PLACED TOGETHER AND BONDED BY HEAT, PRESSURE, AND ADHESIVES: PLASTIC, PLYWOOD, AND COMBINED MATERIALS SUCH AS WOOD AND METAL.

PLASTIC COMPOUNDS ARE CONVERTED TO SHEET MATERIAL BY PRESSING BETWEEN A SERIES OF ROLLERS. TEXTURES CAN BE APPLIED BY THE ROLLERS: PLASTIC AND GLASS.

SHEET MATERIAL FORMED BY PRESSURE: PLASTIC AND GLASS.

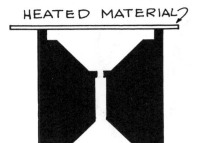

HEATED MATERIAL?

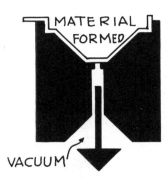

MATERIAL FORMED

VACUUM

MATERIAL COOLED

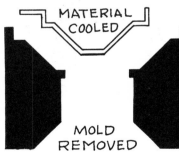

MOLD REMOVED

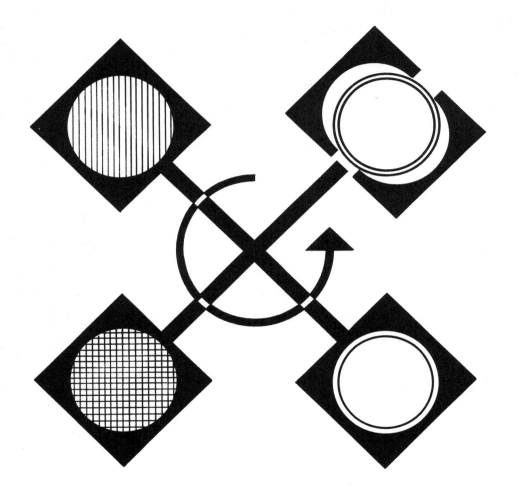

EXPANDABLE PELLETS?

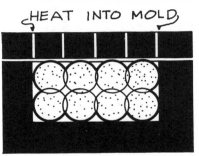

HEAT INTO MOLD

EXPANDED PELLETS

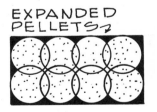

A HEATED PLASTIC SHEET IS PULLED INTO A MOLD BY A VACUUM. WHEN THE MATERIAL COOLS THE MOLD IS REMOVED: PLASTICS

A ROTATING MOLDING MACHINE CONVEYS THE MATERIAL FROM LOADING THROUGH A HEATING CYCLE TO COOLING AND UNLOADING. ROTATION CAUSES THE MATERIAL TO ADHERE TO THE WALLS OF THE MOLD FORMING A HOLLOW OBJECT: PLASTICS.

EXPANDABLE PELLETS ARE PLACED IN A MOLD. HEAT IS INTRODUCED. THE PELLETS EXPAND AND FILL THE MOLD: PLASTICS.

# LIGHT IS RADIANT ENERGY

## THAT AFFECTS THE

**LUMINOUS**
AN OBJECT
THAT EMITS
LIGHT IS
LUMINOUS

**BRIGHTNESS**
THE AMOUNT OF
ENERGY SENT
TO THE EYE

**an object is visible only
when light comes from
it to the eye**

**ILLUMINATED**
AN OBJECT THAT
REFLECTS LIGHT

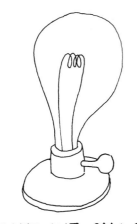

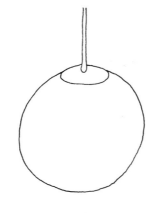

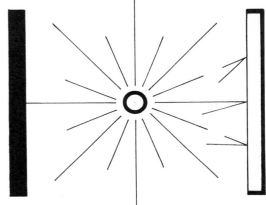

AN OPAQUE OBJECT THAT REFLECTS LIGHT IS A REFLECTOR

WHAT WE CAN SEE THROUGH IS **TRANSPARENT**

WHAT EMITS LIGHT BUT WE CAN NOT SEE THE SOURCE OF THE LIGHT IS **TRANSLUCENT**

WHAT NO LIGHT PASSES THROUGH IS **OPAQUE**

AN OPAQUE OBJECT THAT ABSORBS LIGHT IS AN ABSORBER

**light passing through a medium of uniform density travels in a straight line**

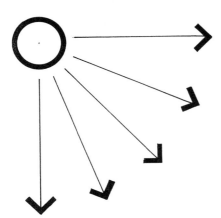

AN OPAQUE OBJECT IN THE PATH OF LIGHT CAUSES SHADOW

FOR THIS REASON IT IS IMPOSSIBLE TO SEE BEHIND OPAQUE OBJECTS

LIGHT DOES NOT BEND AROUND IT

BRIGHT SHINY OBJECTS ARE GOOD REFLECTORS

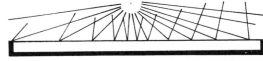

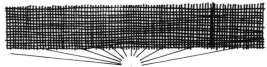

BLACK ROUGH OBJECTS ARE GOOD ABSORBERS

51

# MEASURING RADIANT ENERGY

MEANS OF EVALUATING THE POWER OF LIGHT

INTENSITY OF ILLUMINATION QUANTITY OF LIGHT ON A UNIT AREA

CANDLE POWER

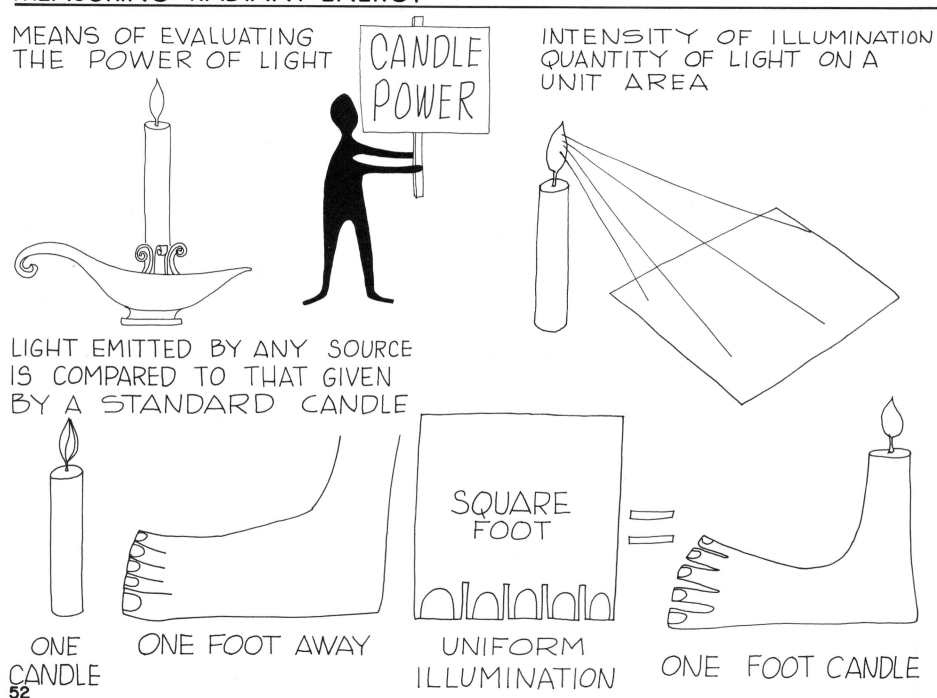

LIGHT EMITTED BY ANY SOURCE IS COMPARED TO THAT GIVEN BY A STANDARD CANDLE

ONE CANDLE

ONE FOOT AWAY

SQUARE FOOT

UNIFORM ILLUMINATION

ONE FOOT CANDLE

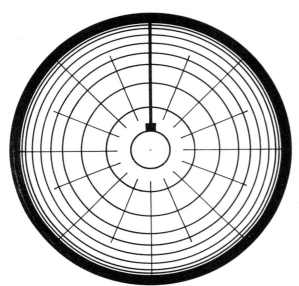

LIGHT FROM A POINT SOURCE RADIATES EQUALLY IN ALL DIRECTIONS AND SPREADS OVER A LARGER AREA AS IT MOVES AWAY FROM THE SOURCE

THE AREA ILLUMINATED IS THE AREA OF AN EXPANDING SPHERE
$A = 4\pi r$

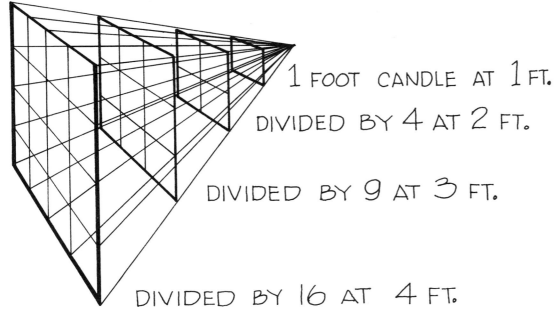

1 FOOT CANDLE AT 1 FT.

DIVIDED BY 4 AT 2 FT.

DIVIDED BY 9 AT 3 FT.

DIVIDED BY 16 AT 4 FT.

$$\text{FOOT CANDLES} = \frac{\text{CANDLE POWER OF SOURCE}}{\text{SQUARE OF DISTANCE FROM SOURCE}}$$

# LUMEN
UNIT OF LUMINOUS FLUX EQUAL TO ONE FOOT CANDLE

# EFFICIENCY
OF A LIGHT SOURCE IS DETERMINED BY THE AMOUNT OF LIGHT PRODUCED PER WATT OF ELECTRICAL POWER USED

 CANDLE
0.1 LUMENS PER WATT

 TUNGSTEN LAMPS
20 LUMENS PER WATT

FLUORESCENT LAMP
80 LUMENS PER WATT

THESE WATT AMOUNTS ARE APPROXIMATE

**53**

# SHADOWS AND BOUNCING LIGHT

● POINT SOURCE - SIZE OF LIGHT
SOURCE IS LESS THAN 1/5
ITS DISTANCE FROM
THE ILLUMINATED
OBJECT

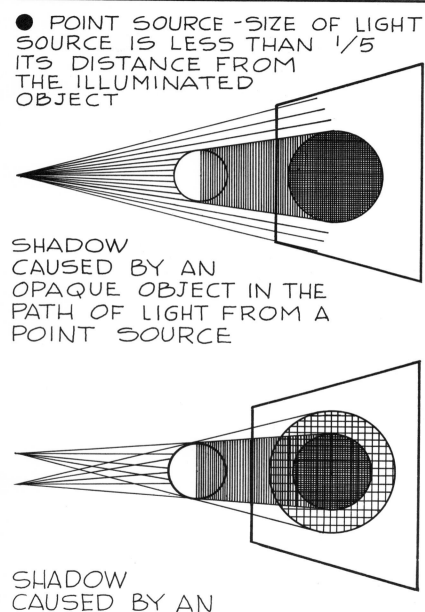

SHADOW
CAUSED BY AN
OPAQUE OBJECT IN THE
PATH OF LIGHT FROM A
POINT SOURCE

SHADOW
CAUSED BY AN
OPAQUE OBJECT IN THE
PATH OF A LARGE LIGHT
SOURCE

BLACK OBJECTS ARE VISIBLE WHEN
SURROUNDING OBJECTS REFLECT LIGHT
TO CREATE CONTRAST

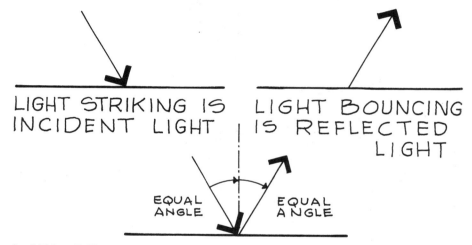

LIGHT STRIKING IS
INCIDENT LIGHT

LIGHT BOUNCING
IS REFLECTED
LIGHT

EQUAL
ANGLE

EQUAL
ANGLE

## LAW OF REFLECTION

A LINE DRAWN PERPENDICULAR TO THE REFLECTED SURFACE AT THE

POINT THE INCIDENT RAY STRIKES IS CALLED THE NORMAL.

THE ANGLE BETWEEN THE NORMAL AND THE INCIDENT RAY IS

THE ANGLE OF INCIDENCE. THE ANGLE OF REFLECTION IS THE ANGLE

MADE BY THE NORMAL AND THE REFLECTED RAY. THE LAW STATES:

THE ANGLE OF INCIDENCE EQUALS THE ANGLE OF REFLECTION.

because of the law of reflection we can use light to do what we want it to do

REFLECTORS CONTROL THE DISTRIBUTION OF LIGHT WITH THEIR CONTOURS AND THE LOCATION OF THE LIGHT SOURCE

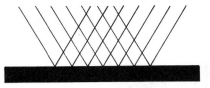

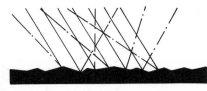

SMOOTH SURFACES REFLECT RAYS UNIFORMLY

ROUGH SURFACES DIFFUSE RAYS

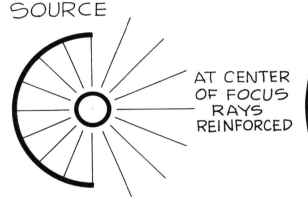

AT CENTER OF FOCUS RAYS REINFORCED

AHEAD OF FOCUS RAYS JUMBLED

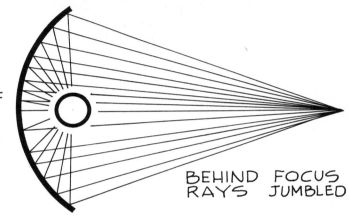

BEHIND FOCUS RAYS JUMBLED

## CIRCULAR REFLECTORS

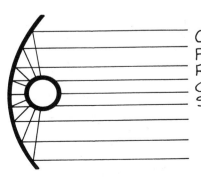

CENTER OF FOCUS RAYS CONTROLLED STRONG

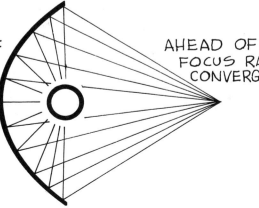

AHEAD OF FOCUS RAYS CONVERGE

BEHIND FOCUS RAYS SPREAD

## PARABOLIC REFLECTORS

# EYE COMFORT AND STIMULATION

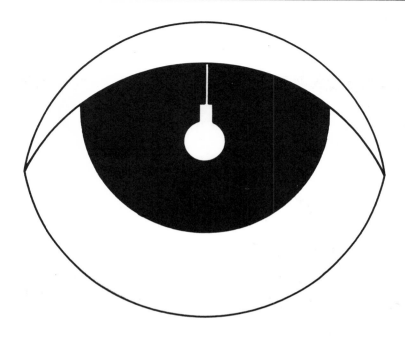

ROOM LIGHTING LEVELS DEPEND UPON THE AMOUNT OF LIGHT INTRODUCED AND THE CAPACITY OF THE ROOM SURFACES TO REFLECT AND ABSORB IT. LIGHTING LEVELS CAN NOT BE TRANSLATED INTO BRIGHTNESS WITHOUT CONSIDERING THE COLOR SCHEME OF THE SPACE AND ITS REFLECTING QUALITIES.

THE LEVELS OF ARTIFICIAL LIGHTING ARE VERY LOW COMPARED TO DAYLIGHT. THE DIFFERENCE BETWEEN EXTERIOR AND INTERIOR ILLUMINATION CAN THEREFORE EASILY BE THE SOURCE OF GLARING CONTRAST.

WHEN DAYLIGHT IS INTRODUCED INTO AN INTERIOR THE ARTIFICIAL LIGHTING LEVEL MUST BE RAISED IN THE AREA OF BRIGHT DAYLIGHT. A ROOM WITH NO WINDOWS CAN APPEAR BRIGHTLY LIT AT 30 LUMENS PER SQUARE FOOT. A WINDOW INTRODUCING 200 LUMENS PER SQUARE FOOT MAKES THE SAME ROOM APPEAR GLOOMY BY CONTRAST.

THE EYE PREFERS EVEN LIGHTING, WITH A MINIMUM OF CONTRAST BETWEEN THE BRIGHTNESS OF THE ROOM SURFACES AND THE LIGHTING FIXTURES.

OBJECTS TO WHICH THE DESIGNER WISHES TO DRAW ATTENTION SHOULD BE LIT MORE BRIGHTLY THAN THEIR SURROUNDINGS, BUT A POOL OF LIGHT SURROUNDED BY GLOOM IS NOT AN IDEAL SOLUTION. THE SURROUNDING ROOM SHOULD NOT BE BRIGHTER THAN THE WORKING SURFACES.

THE EYE IS ATTRACTED TO ANY SOURCE OF LIGHT AND TO STRONG CONTRASTS. BRIGHT LIGHTS AND THE STRONGEST TONAL CONTRASTS MUST OCCUR IN THE AREA THE DESIGNER WANTS PEOPLE TO LOOK AT.

THREE THINGS TO REMEMBER

1. THE EYE IS MOST COMFORTABLE IN EVEN LIGHTING.

2. THE EYE WORKS BEST WHEN THE WORK IS MORE BRIGHTLY LIT THAN ITS SURROUNDINGS.

3. THE EYE IS STIMULATED BY CONTRASTS OF TONE AND SPARKLE.

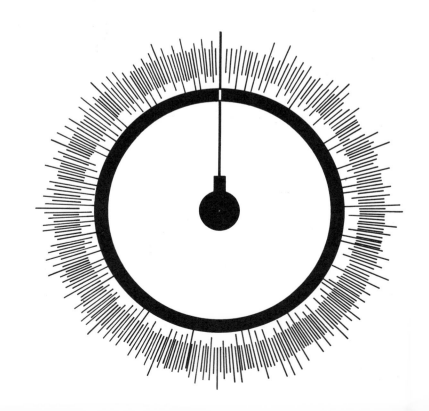

EVERY ACTIVITY THAT TAKES PLACE IN THE INTERIOR MUST HAVE LIGHT
OF THE RIGHT KIND, INTENSITY, AND DIRECTION. WHEN ROOM LIGHTING
CHANGES, COLORS CHANGE OR DISAPPEAR, OBJECTS BECOME MORE OR LESS
IMPORTANT IN THE ROOM. A DIFFERENT LIGHTING SCHEME PRODUCES A
COMPLETELY DIFFERENT ROOM.

THERE ARE TWO KINDS OF ROOM LIGHT THAT MUST BE CONSIDERED, DAY-
LIGHT AND ARTIFICIAL LIGHT. THE DIFFERENCE BETWEEN THESE TWO KINDS
OF LIGHT FORCES THE DESIGNER TO MAKE A DECISION BETWEEN THE RELATION
OF DAY AND NIGHT LIGHTING AT THE VERY BEGINNING OF THE DESIGN.

THE TWO LIGHTINGS CAN BE DESIGNED AS TOTALLY DIFFERENT, OR
ARTIFICIAL LIGHT CAN BE DESIGNED TO FALL FROM THE SAME DIRECTION AS
DAYLIGHT. ARTIFICIAL LIGHT CAN NEVER BE AS VARIED OR OF THE SAME
INTENSITY AS DAYLIGHT. AS HUMAN LIVING SPACES CONTINUALLY DWINDLE IN
SIZE, LIGHTING SCHEMES CAN BE A MEANS OF ALTERING SPATIAL APPEARANCES
AND ADDING INTEREST.

LIGHTING DESIGN IS RESPONSIBLE FOR THE MOOD OF A ROOM BUT ITS
DESIGN IS ANYTHING BUT MOOD. THE SUBTLETIES OF A GOOD LIGHTING SCHEME
ARE THE RESULT OF CAREFUL CALCULATION, EXPERIENCE, AND KNOWLEDGE.

WHAT HAPPENS TO THE EYE HAPPENS TO THE BRAIN. THE TWO ARE CLOSELY
CONNECTED. IF THE EYE IS UNCOMFORTABLE WE HAVE AN UNEASY FEELING ABOUT
THE INTERIOR ITSELF.

THE EYE IS DAZZLED WHEN IT LOOKS AT BRIGHT SUNLIGHT AFTER ADJUST-
ING TO A DARK ROOM. TO COME INTO A DARK ROOM FROM BRIGHT SUNLIGHT
CAUSES TEMPORARY BLINDNESS. THE EYE CANNOT ADAPT IMMEDIATELY TO
EXTREME LIGHTING LEVELS. ANY BRIGHTNESS ABOVE THE LEVEL TO WHICH THE
EYE HAS ADAPTED IS A POTENTIAL CAUSE OF GLARE. THEREFORE, WHEN A LEVEL
OF LIGHT IS ESTABLISHED IN A ROOM, THE BRIGHTNESS OF INDIVIDUAL PATCHES
OR ACCENTS OF LIGHT MUST BE FAIRLY NEAR TO THE GENERAL BRIGHTNESS LEVEL.

# LIGHTING SYMBOLS

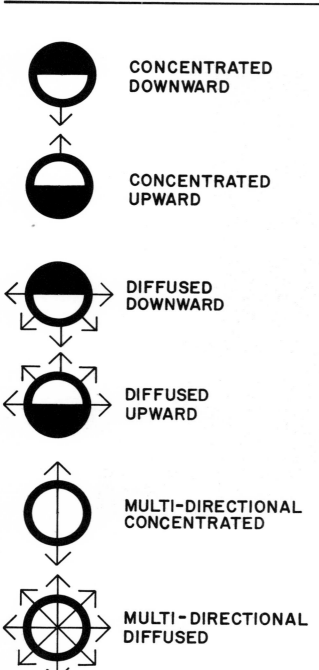

CONCENTRATED
DOWNWARD

CONCENTRATED
UPWARD

DIFFUSED
DOWNWARD

DIFFUSED
UPWARD

MULTI-DIRECTIONAL
CONCENTRATED

MULTI-DIRECTIONAL
DIFFUSED

58

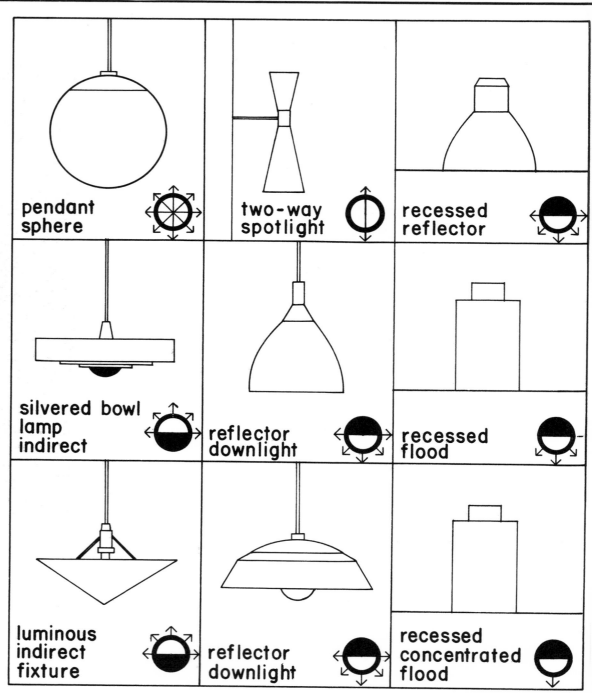

pendant
sphere

two-way
spotlight

recessed
reflector

silvered bowl
lamp
indirect

reflector
downlight

recessed
flood

luminous
indirect
fixture

reflector
downlight

recessed
concentrated
flood

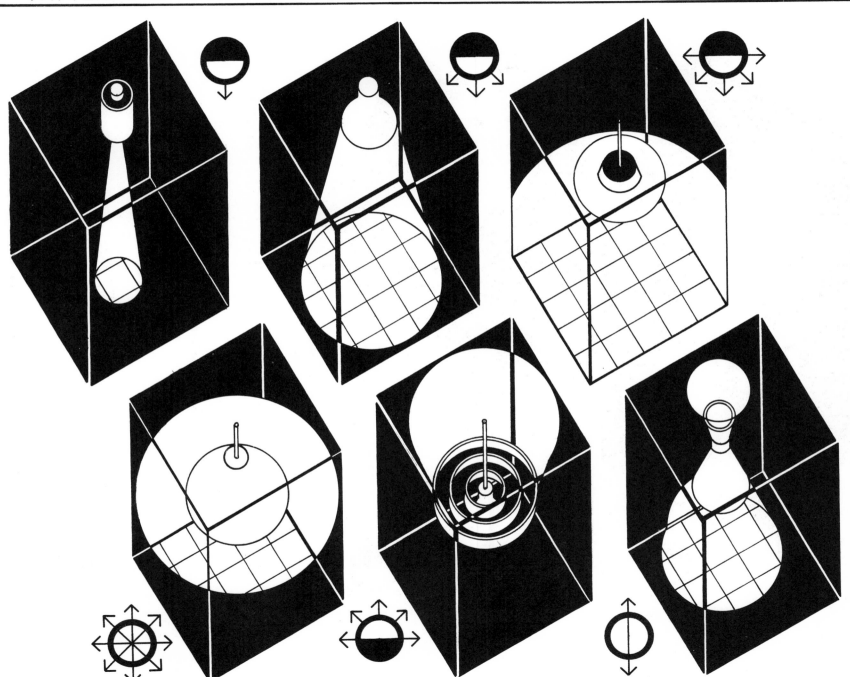

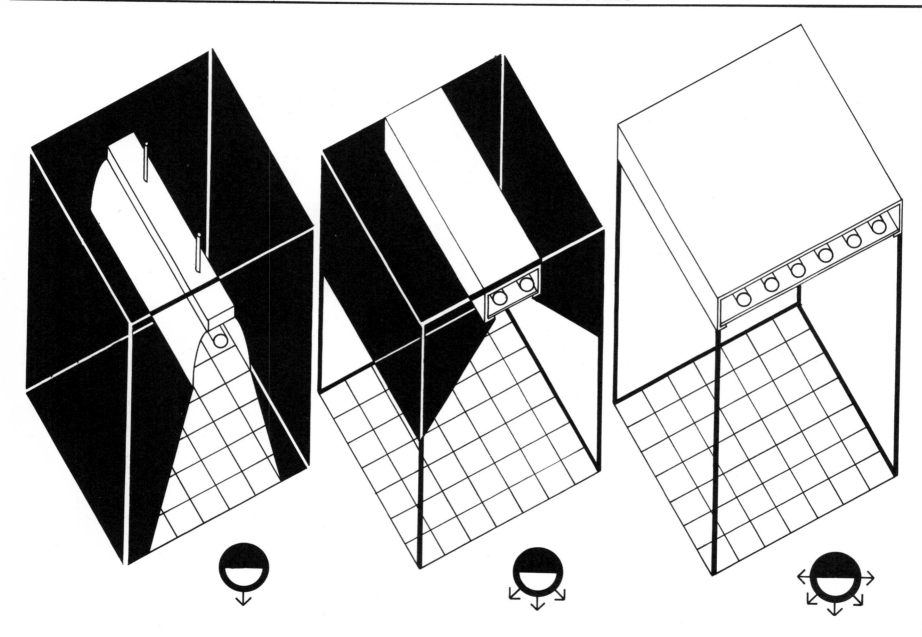

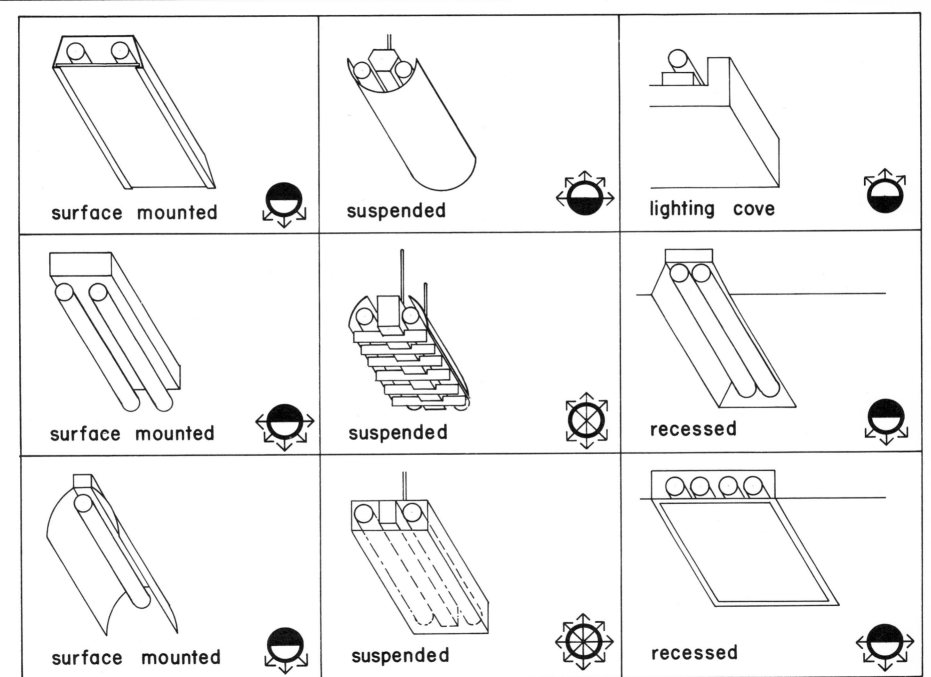

surface mounted

suspended

lighting cove

surface mounted

suspended

recessed

surface mounted

suspended

recessed

# LIGHTING DESIGN

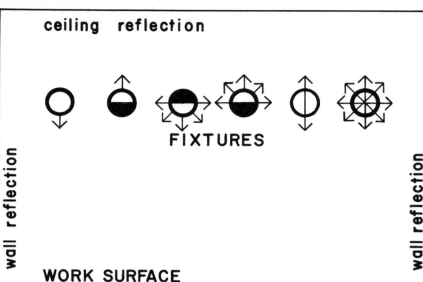

ceiling reflection

wall reflection

FIXTURES

wall reflection

WORK SURFACE

floor reflection

A WORKING METHOD OF DESIGNING LIGHTING IS TO FIRST DETERMINE THE LIGHT LEVELS REQUIRED FOR EACH SEEING TASK IN THE SPACE AND THEN SIMPLIFY WITHOUT LOSS OF CONVENIENCE. DETERMINE THE REFLECTING QUALITIES OF FLOORS AND CEILING. THE LEVEL OF REFLECTED LIGHT SHOULD BE JUST BELOW THE WORKING LEVEL.

AFTER PLANNING WORKING LIGHTS AND MAKING CERTAIN THAT THE WALLS AND CEILINGS REFLECT ENOUGH LIGHT TO AVOID GLOOM, THE SCHEME IS COMPLETE. TO CHECK YOURSELF MOVE AROUND THE SPACE AND CONSIDER WHETHER THE LIGHTS IN DISTANT PARTS OF THE ROOM WILL BE IN THE LINE OF VISION AND THUS PRODUCE GLARE.

CONSIDER THE PLAN OF THE LIGHT SOURCES. WHAT PATTERN DO THEY MAKE IN ISOLATION? LIGHTING ACCENTS SHOULD COINCIDE WITH ACCENTS OF THE TOTAL PLAN.

ARTIFICIAL LIGHT IS DESIGNED AND CALCULATED AS AN INTEGRAL ELEMENT OF THE TOTAL DESIGN. THERE ARE ESSENTIALLY THREE PRIMARY FACTORS TO CON-SIDER: THE FIXTURE, ITS RELATION TO THE WORKING SURFACES, AND ITS RE-LATION TO THE REFLECTING SURFACES OF THE SPACE. LIGHT ROOM SURFACES REFLECT LIGHT; THEREFORE LESS ILLUMINATION IS NEEDED AND GLARE IS REDUCED BY LIGHTING SOURCES.

LIGHTING MUST BE DESIGNED FOR SEEING TASKS. UNIFORM LIGHTING IS USED FOR UNIFORM ACTIVITIES SUCH AS FACTORY OR OFFICE WORK. IN THE HOME THE TASKS DIFFER AS IN SCHOOLWORK, HOBBIES, READING, COOKING, AND WATCHING TELEVISION; THEREFORE LIGHTING MUST BE VARIED.

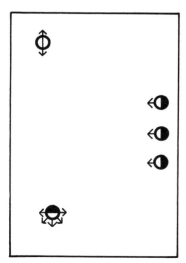

**PLAN
DINING ROOM**

**PLAN
FACTORY WORKROOM**

THE INTERIOR DESIGNER WILL FIND THAT IT IS IMPOSSIBLE TO IMITATE EXTERIOR DAYLIGHT IN THE INTERIOR. THE COLOR OF DAYLIGHT CHANGES ALMOST MOMENTARILY ACCORDING TO THE COMPOSITION OF THE ATMOSPHERE AND THE INTERREFLECTION OF OBJECTS IN THE OUTSIDE ENVIRONMENT SUCH AS GREEN GRASS, COLORED BUILDINGS, AND PAVEMENT. DAYLIGHT CHANGES WITH THE PASSAGE OF CLOUDS, POLLUTION, AND TIME OF DAY. TYPICAL DAYLIGHT BEGINS WITH THE PURPLE AND DEEP RED SUNRISE AND CONTINUES THROUGH A RANGE OF ORANGES AND YELLOWS TO BLUE—WHITE SKYLIGHT. THEN THE CYCLE REVERSES ITSELF AND PROCEEDS THROUGH THE ORANGE, RED, AND PURPLE OF SUNSET TO DARKNESS.

A WEAK IMITATION OF THIS RANGE OF COLORS IS AVAILABLE TO THE INTERIOR DESIGNER THROUGH MAN—MADE LAMPS, BUT THE COLORS NEVER DUPLICATE THOSE OF NATURE NOR DO THEY EVER REACH ITS INTENSITY.

TUNGSTEN LAMPS ARE RED AND BURN LIKE THE SUN. THE GASEOUS DISCHARGE LAMPS, SUCH AS FLUORESCENT, MERCURY VAPOR, AND NEON LAMPS THAT PASS AN ELECTRIC ARC THROUGH VARIOUS GASES AND REFLECT ON PHOSPHORS, RIVAL AND IMITATE THE RANGE OF DAYLIGHT.

THE PASSAGE OF CURRENT THROUGH NEON PRODUCES RED; THROUGH HELIUM, A PALE GREENISH YELLOW; THROUGH MERCURY VAPOR, BLUE—GREEN; THROUGH ARGON, BLUISH PURPLE; THROUGH SODIUM VAPOR, YELLOW. THESE ARE THE RANGES OF COLOR THE INTERIOR DESIGNER HAS TO WORK WITH. NONETHELESS THE BEST POLICY IS TO FIND LIGHT AS NEUTRAL AS POSSIBLE, COMING AS CLOSE AS POSSIBLE TO THE BLUE—WHITE LIGHT OF MIDDAY.

THE DESIGNER CAN EMPLOY A RANGE OF CHOICES TO KINDLE INTEREST IN THE INTERIOR. A POOL OF LIGHT ON A WALL, SCALLOPED EDGES FROM DOWN—LIGHTS, A HANGING PENDENT OF LIGHT, OR OPAQUE GLASS ADD CHARACTER AND SERVE TO EMPHASIZE THE DESIGNER'S INTENTIONS. THE CLASSIC DEVICE OF GILDED MIRRORS, WHICH REFLECT LIGHT AND ADD ROOM DEPTH, HAS BEEN USED FOR SEVERAL HUNDRED YEARS. THE MODERN VERSION IS TO HIGHLIGHT A WORK OF ART OR ORNAMENT WITH A SPOTLIGHT.

WHEN INDIRECT LIGHTING OF WALLS AND CEILINGS IS DESIGNED, THEN OTHER PARTS OF THE ROOM SEEM DIMLY LIT IN COMPARISON. ONE OR TWO DIRECT LIGHTING FIXTURES TO ADD ACCENT WILL RELIEVE THIS CONDITION. IT IS DIFFICULT TO ILLUMINATE ANY ROOM EXCEPT A CLOSET SUCCESSFULLY WITH A SINGLE LIGHT SOURCE. SEVERAL SMALLER LAMPS WILL DO MORE FOR THE SPACE AND CREATE MORE INTEREST THAN ONE LARGE ONE.

TUNGSTEN AND FLUORESCENT LIGHT SOURCES SHOULD NOT BE CONSIDERED AS ALTERNATIVES. THEY SHOULD BE USED TO COMPLEMENT EACH OTHER. ENTIRE WALLS AND CEILINGS CAN BE ILLUMINATED WITH FLUORESCENT TUBES. HOWEVER, A UNIFORMLY LIT LUMINOUS CEILING, NO MATTER HOW BRIGHT, MAKES THE INTERIOR SEEM LIKE A DULL DAY COMPARED TO THE DAYLIGHT OUTSIDE. IT IS BEST TO WORK WITH CONTRASTS AND ACCENTS, CONSIDERING THE INTERIOR AS AN ENVIRONMENT COMPLETE IN ITSELF.

# SOUND IS VIBRATION ENERGY

SOUND IS THE RESULT OF VIBRATION—THE MEDIUM TRANSMITTING THE SOUND—AIR, WATER, STEEL—VIBRATES

## THAT DRUMS ON THE EAR

THE SOUND SOURCE PUSHES VIBRATIONS THROUGH THE AIR TO THE EAR. THE EAR—DRUM VIBRATES. THE BRAIN TRANSLATES THE VIBRATION INTO AUDIBLE SOUND.

CORK, SAWDUST, PUTTY DO NOT VIBRATE AND DO NOT TRANSMIT SOUND

A VACUUM DOES NOT TRANSMIT SOUND—THERE IS NO MATTER IN THE VACUUM TO VIBRATE

THE SOUND WAVE MOVES PARALLEL TO THE DIRECTION IN WHICH THE TRANSMITTING PARTICLES VIBRATE AND IS CALLED A LONGITUDINAL WAVE. THE MEDIUM THAT TRANSMITS THE WAVES MUST BE ELASTIC, THAT IS, ONE THAT IS DISPLACED BY THE APPLICATION OF A FORCE AND RETURNS TO ITS ORIGINAL POSITION OR SHAPE AS SOON AS THE FORCE IS REMOVED.

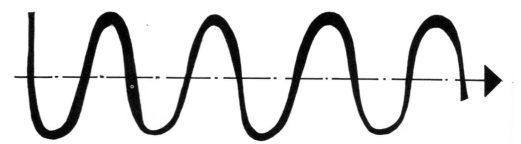

# VELOCITY

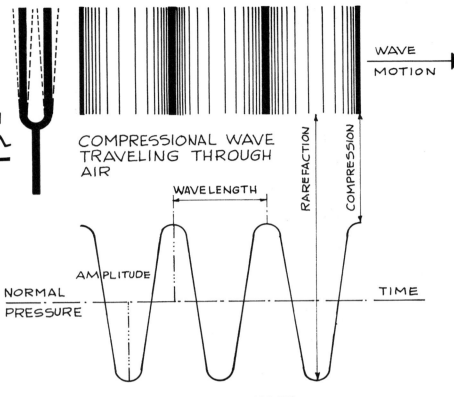

COMPRESSIONAL WAVE
TRAVELING THROUGH
AIR

WAVE MOTION

RAREFACTION

COMPRESSION

WAVELENGTH

AMPLITUDE

NORMAL
PRESSURE

TIME

## GRAPH OF WAVE

VELOCITY DEPENDS ON THE DENSITY AND ELASTICITY OF THE TRANSMITTING
MEDIUM.

AIR — 1,090 FT./SEC. (AT 0° C.)

WATER — 4800 FT./SEC. (AT 0° C.)

STEEL — 15,000 FT./SEC. (AT 0° C.)

THE DENSER THE MEDIUM, THE FASTER THE SOUND TRAVELS.  VELOCITY IN
AIR IS AFFECTED BY THE TEMPERATURE.  A CHANGE IN TEMPERATURE CAUSES
A CHANGE IN THE DENSITY OF ALL GASES.

VELOCITY  =  1,090 +  2 X °C.

ALL SOUNDS TRAVEL WITH THE SAME VELOCITY IN A GIVEN MEDIUM.  A
TUNING FORK MAKING 226 VIBRATIONS EACH SECOND PRODUCES 226 SOUND
WAVES EACH SECOND.  THE FIRST WAVE TRAVELS THE DISTANCE OF 1,190 FEET
IN ONE SECOND AND IS FOLLOWED BY 225 WAVES IN THE FORM OF A WAVE
TRAIN.  DIVIDE VELOCITY BY FREQUENCY (NUMBER OF WAVES IN ONE SECOND)
TO OBTAIN WAVE LENGTH.

WAVE LENGTH  = $\dfrac{\text{VELOCITY}}{\text{FREQUENCY}}$  = $\dfrac{1,190}{226}$ = 5 FEET

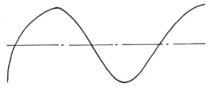
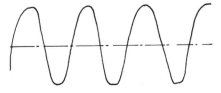

## LOW        HIGH

**the greater the frequency of waves the
shorter the wave length**

WAVE LENGTH  THE DISTANCE BETWEEN TWO CORRESPONDING POINTS ON
THE SOUND WAVE.  COMPRESSION CAUSES AN INCREASE IN NORMAL AIR
PRESSURE WHICH IS THE CREST OF THE WAVE.  RAREFACTION CAUSES A
MOMENTARY DECREASE IN AIR PRESSURE WHICH IS THE TROUGH.

FREQUENCY  THE DISTANCE BETWEEN ANY TWO CORRESPONDING POINTS ON
THE SOUND WAVE.  THE WAVE LENGTH IS THE LENGTH OF ONE COMPLETE
WAVE DUE TO ONE COMPLETE VIBRATION.

FREQUENCY  THE NUMBER OF COMPLETE VIBRATIONS IN ONE SECOND.

AMPLITUDE  MAXIMUM DISPLACEMENT WHEN THE PRESSURE CHANGE IS
GREATEST.

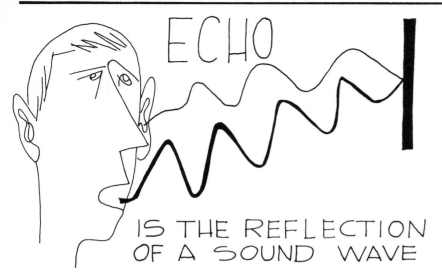

## ECHO

## IS THE REFLECTION OF A SOUND WAVE

**HARD** **SOFT**

## PERIOD OF REVERBERATION

IS THE LENGTH OF TIME REFLECTED SOUND CAN BE HEARD.

EQ.

EQ.

SOUND, LIKE LIGHT, IS REFLECTED ACCORDING TO THE CONVENTIONAL LAWS OF REFLECTION: THE ANGLE OF INCIDENCE EQUALS THE ANGLE OF REFLECTION.

AS A SOUNDWAVE MOVES AWAY FROM THE SOURCE, THE LOUDNESS DECREASES. THE SOUND BECOMES WEAKER BUT THE FREQUENCY AND WAVE LENGTH REMAIN THE SAME.

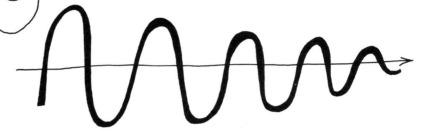

LOUDNESS CAN BE INCREASED BY FORCED VIBRATION. A VIBRATING OBJECT IN CONTACT WITH A HARD SURFACE THAT VIBRATES AT THE SAME FREQUENCY WILL SET A LARGER MASS OF AIR INTO VIBRATION AND INCREASE LOUDNESS.

ACTUAL PHYSICAL CONTACT IS NECESSARY TO PRODUCE FORCED VIBRATION.

VIBRATING ENERGY FROM ONE BODY WILL CAUSE A NEARBY BODY TO VIBRATE WITHOUT CONTACT IF BOTH OBJECTS HAVE THE SAME FUNDAMENTAL FREQUENCY OF VIBRATION.

# PITCH

DEPENDS ON SOUND-WAVE FREQUENCY. THE
AVERAGE EAR RESPONDS TO FREQUENCIES OF
FROM 20 TO 20,000 WAVES EACH SECOND,
THE CORRESPONDING WAVE LENGTHS FROM 3/4
INCH TO 9 1/2 FEET LONG.

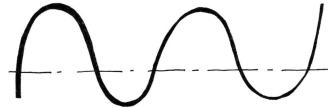

## LOW FREQUENCY
## LOW PITCH

## HIGH FREQUENCY
## HIGH PITCH

INTENSITY OF A SOUND VARIES DIRECTLY AS
THE AMPLITUDE OF THE SOUND WAVE. THUNDER
IS LOW PITCHED BUT VERY LOUD BECAUSE OF
THE LARGE MASS OF AIR SET INTO VIBRATION.

# LOUDNESS

## SMALL AMPLITUDE
## WEAK SOUND

## LARGE AMPLITUDE
## STRONG SOUND

LOUDNESS OR INTENSITY DEPENDS ON WAVE ENERGY. TO MAKE A SOUND OF A CERTAIN
FREQUENCY TWICE AS LOUD IT IS NECESSARY TO INCREASE THE PRESSURE 100 TIMES.
TO TRIPLE LOUDNESS THE ENERGY MUST BE INCREASED 1,000 TIMES.

| INTENSITY | PRESSURE LEVEL (DECIBELS) | SOUND |
|---|---|---|
| 100,000,000,000,000 | 140 | JET ENGINE |
| 10,000,000,000,000 | 130 | GUNFIRE (THRESHOLD OF PAIN) |
| 1,000,000,000,000 | 120 | ELEVATED TRAIN |
| 100,000,000,000 | 110 | AIRPLANE ENGINE |
| 10,000,000,000 | 100 | LOUD BAND |
| 1,000,000,000 | 90 | SYMPHONY ORCHESTRA |
| 100,000,000 | 80 | AUTOMOBILE ENGINE |
| 10,000,000 | 70 | LOUD CONVERSATION |
| 1,000,000 | 60 | OFFICE NOISE |
| 100,000 | 50 | OFFICE NOISE |
| 10,000 | 40 | PRIVATE OFFICE |
| 1,000 | 30 | BEDROOM |
| 100 | 20 | EMPTY THEATER |
| 10 | 10 | FALLING LEAVES |
| 0 | 1 | THRESHOLD OF HEARING |

**67**

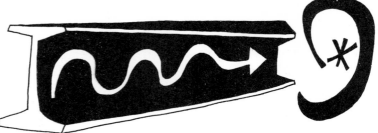

## AIR-BORNE
## VIBRATIONS IN THE AIR

## BUILDING-BORNE
## VIBRATIONS IN BUILDING MATERIALS

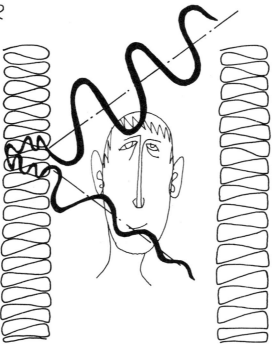
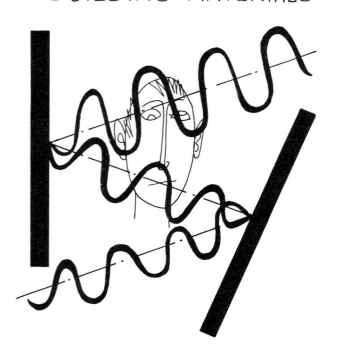

AIR-BORNE SOUND WILL LOSE ITS ENERGY THROUGH SUCCESSIVE RE-VERBERATIONS AS IT IS REFLECTED FROM ONE HARD SURFACE TO THE OTHER. THE EFFECT CAN BE VERY UNPLEASANT FOR ROOM OCCUPANTS.

SOFT MATERIALS ON ROOM SURFACES ABSORB AND DISSIPATE SOUND ENERGY. THEY DO NOT TRANSFER SOUND ENERGY BY VIBRATION.

UNPARALLEL HARD SURFACES DEFLECT SOUND.

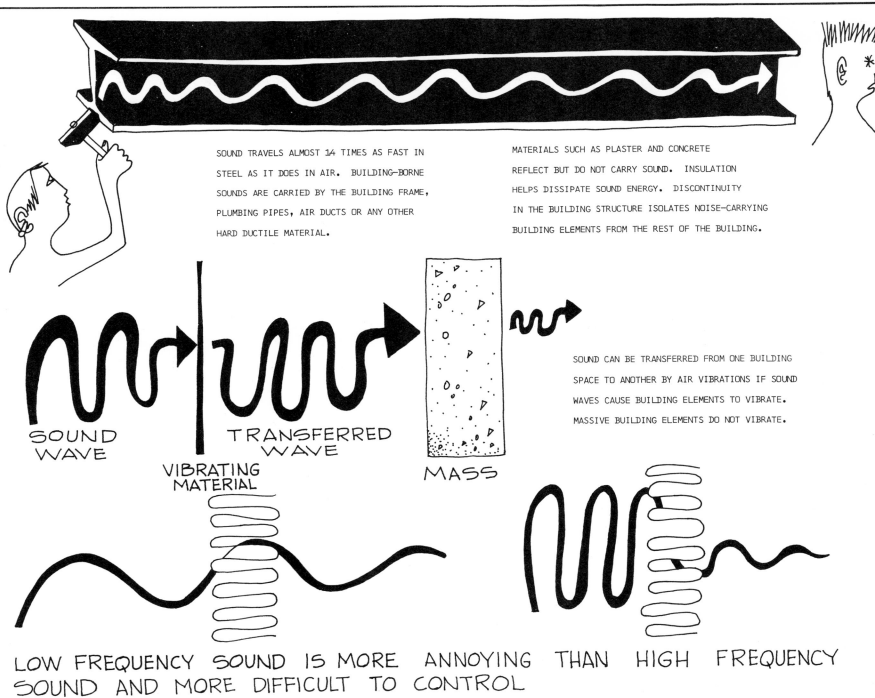

SOUND TRAVELS ALMOST 14 TIMES AS FAST IN STEEL AS IT DOES IN AIR. BUILDING-BORNE SOUNDS ARE CARRIED BY THE BUILDING FRAME, PLUMBING PIPES, AIR DUCTS OR ANY OTHER HARD DUCTILE MATERIAL.

MATERIALS SUCH AS PLASTER AND CONCRETE REFLECT BUT DO NOT CARRY SOUND. INSULATION HELPS DISSIPATE SOUND ENERGY. DISCONTINUITY IN THE BUILDING STRUCTURE ISOLATES NOISE-CARRYING BUILDING ELEMENTS FROM THE REST OF THE BUILDING.

SOUND CAN BE TRANSFERRED FROM ONE BUILDING SPACE TO ANOTHER BY AIR VIBRATIONS IF SOUND WAVES CAUSE BUILDING ELEMENTS TO VIBRATE. MASSIVE BUILDING ELEMENTS DO NOT VIBRATE.

SOUND WAVE

TRANSFERRED WAVE

VIBRATING MATERIAL

MASS

LOW FREQUENCY SOUND IS MORE ANNOYING THAN HIGH FREQUENCY SOUND AND MORE DIFFICULT TO CONTROL

# NOISE INVASION OF INTERIOR SPACE

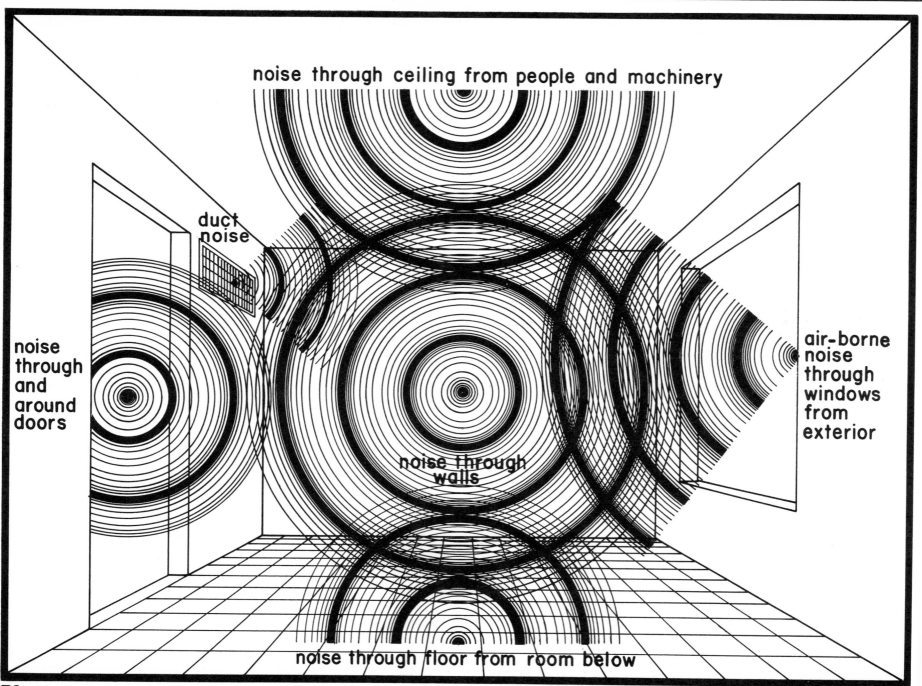

noise through ceiling from people and machinery

duct noise

noise through and around doors

air-borne noise through windows from exterior

noise through walls

noise through floor from room below

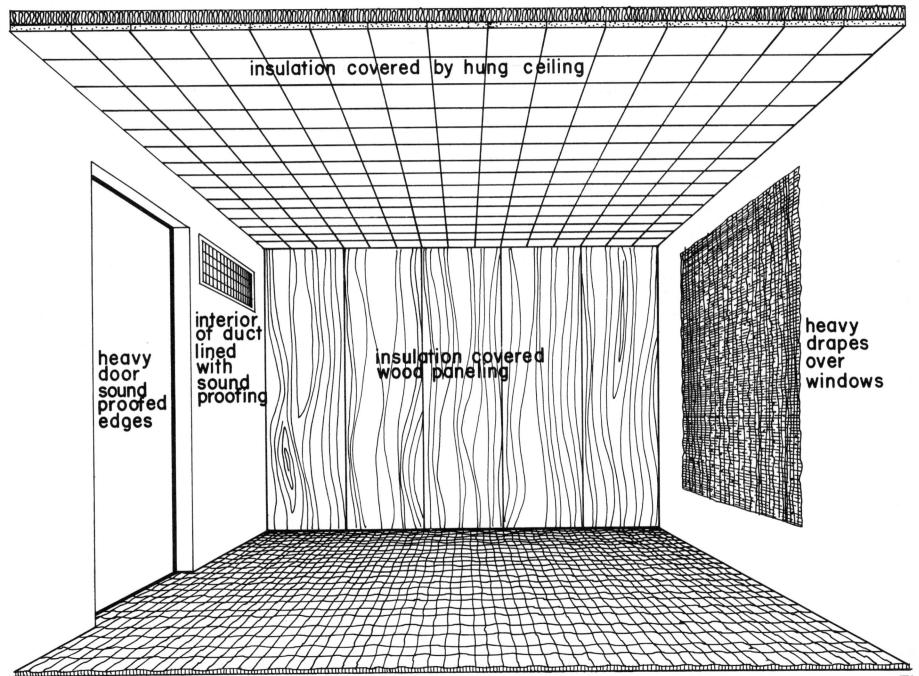

insulation covered by hung ceiling

heavy door sound proofed edges

interior of duct lined with sound proofing

insulation covered wood paneling

heavy drapes over windows

carpet and padding

# SOUNDS AND SOLUTIONS

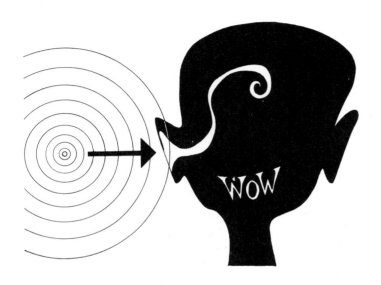

VIBRATIONS IN THE BUILDING FRAME CAN BE CONTROLLED BY MASS, DISCONTINUITY, AND INSULATION. SOUND TRAVELS THROUGH THE BUILDING MATERIALS, A BREAK OR DISCONTINUITY DOES NOT TRANSMIT VIBRATION. AIR SPACES ISOLATE ONE PART OF A STRUCTURE FROM THE OTHER AND DO NOT CONVEY SOUND ENERGY DIRECTLY. WEIGHT, MASS, AND STIFFNESS PROVIDE INERTIA TO RESIST SOUND VIBRATION. AS A GENERAL RULE THE GREATER THE MASS, THE GREATER THE REDUCTION IN SOUND TRANSMISSION. A MASSIVE BUILDING ELEMENT, SUCH AS ONE MADE OF STONE OR LEAD, CANNOT BE SET INTO VIBRATING MOTION TO TRANSMIT THE SOUND. BUT THIS IS A COSTLY METHOD OF PREVENTING SOUND AND ADDS TO THE BUILDING WEIGHT. INSULATION IS CHEAPER AND VERY EFFECTIVE.

INSULATION ENCOURAGES THE DISSIPATION OF SOUND ENERGY WITHIN ITS PORES BUT ALSO TRANSMITS SOUND. A COMBINATION OF SOFT INSULATION AND HARD SURFACES CAN BE USED. THE SOUND ENTERS, IS DISSIPATED IN THE OPENINGS, STRIKES THE HARD SURFACE, AND IS FURTHER DISSIPATED AS IT REFLECTS BACK.

LOW FREQUENCY SOUNDS ARE MORE ANNOYING TO THE HUMAN EAR THAN HIGH FREQUENCY AND MORE DIFFICULT TO CONTROL. LOW FREQUENCY WAVES ARE LONGER AND THEREFORE TEND TO PASS THROUGH INSULATING MATERIAL. HIGH FREQUENCY WAVES ARE MORE QUICKLY DISSIPATED.

THE BEST WAY TO HAVE QUIET IS NOT TO MAKE NOISE. THE NEXT BEST IS TO MASK IT WHERE IT HAPPENS AND THE THIRD BEST IS TO ISOLATE NOISY AREAS FROM QUIET ONES.

SOUNDS WHICH BECOME NOISE ARE TRANSMITTED IN A BUILDING IN TWO WAYS, THROUGH THE AIR AND THROUGH THE BUILDING ELEMENTS. MOST NOISE REACHES OUR EARS AS A COMBINATION OF BOTH.

IMPACT NOISE IS SOUND GENERATED BY AN OBJECT STRIKING, VIBRATING, OR SLIDING AGAINST A COMPONENT OF THE BUILDING SUCH AS FOOTSTEPS, MOVING FURNITURE, DROPPED OBJECTS, SLAMMED DOORS, THE VIBRATION OF MECHANICAL EQUIPMENT, OR THE OPERATION OF TYPEWRITERS. IMPACT NOISES SET THE BARRIER BETWEEN SPACES INTO VIBRATION, TRANSMITTING SOUND ON BOTH SIDES.

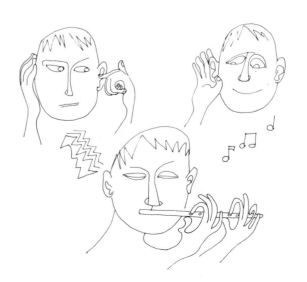

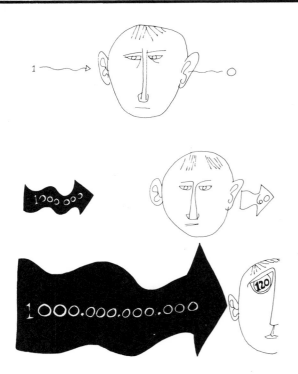

BUT TOO MUCH SOFT POROUS MATERIAL IN A ROOM KILLS ALL SOUND, AND PEOPLE FEEL VERY UNCOMFORTABLE. WE SING IN BATHROOMS BECAUSE THE HARD SURFACES REINFORCE THE SOUND AND MAKE US FEEL IMPORTANT. SPEAKING TO AN AUDIENCE WHERE ONE CANNOT HEAR ONE'S VOICE IS ALSO DISCONCERTING. A CERTAIN AMOUNT OF REVERBERATION IS IMPORTANT.

ROOMS FILLED WITH PEOPLE ACT DIFFERENTLY THAN EMPTY ROOMS. THEY ALSO ACT DIFFERENTLY IN WINTER AND SUMMER BECAUSE OF THE DIFFERENCE IN THE CLOTHING BEING WORN.

AMBIENT NOISE LEVELS SERVE A POSITIVE FUNCTION IN ESTABLISHING AN ARTIFICIAL THRESHOLD THAT WILL MAKE REMOTE OR LOW INTENSITY DISTRACTIONS.

A RULE OF THUMB IS 60 DECIBELS. ABOVE THIS, CONVERSATION BECOMES DIFFICULT. BELOW, AT 20 TO 30 DECIBELS, IT BECOMES TOO OBVIOUS.

IN GENERAL, SPACES THAT CONTAIN OPERATING MACHINES OR INTERACTING GROUPS SHOULD BE TREATED AS ABSORBENT INTERIORS. REFLECTED SOUND IS MINIMIZED BUT NOISE IN THE VICINITY OF THE SOURCE IS UNAFFECTED.

SOUND, LIKE HEAT, WILL TRAVEL THROUGH THE CRACKS FROM EXTERIOR TO INTERIOR IN THE SAME WAY THAT HEAT, IN THE WINTER, WILL PASS THROUGH CRACKS TO THE COLD OUTSIDE. GENERALLY THE SAME MATERIALS USED TO INSULATE A BUILDING AGAINST HEAT LOSS CAN BE USED TO STOP UP BUILDING CRACKS AGAINST SOUND ENTRANCE.

THE TERM NOISY IS A COMPARATIVE DESCRIPTION. IT REFERS TO LACK OF SONIC PRIVACY, NOT TO THE AMOUNT OF SOUND ENERGY. THIS MAY BE DUE TO A SMALL INTRUSION INTO A VERY QUIET SPACE. A CERTAIN NOISE LEVEL IS DESIRABLE TO INSURE PRIVACY. VERY PRIVATE CONVERSATIONS CAN BE HELD IN A NOISY RESTAURANT. THE SURROUNDING NOISE MAKES PRIVATE CONVERSATION POSSIBLE. IT IS NOT POSSIBLE TO CARRY ON A PRIVATE CONVERSATION IN A QUIET CLASSROOM, AS ANY YOUNG STUDENT KNOWS. A MASKING NOISE LEVEL CAN REINFORCE A SENSE OF PRIVACY IN A LARGE SPACE WHERE PEOPLE CAN NOT BE HEARD ABOVE IT.

# PLUMBING clean water in-dirty water out

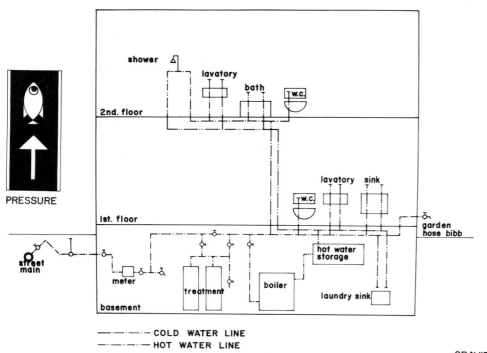

PRESSURE

### RESIDENTIAL WATER SERVICES

— · — · — COLD WATER LINE
—— · ——— · — HOT WATER LINE

CLEAN WATER IS PUSHED INTO THE BUILDING BY THE PRESSURE
IN STREET MAINS. DIRTY WATER LEAVES BY GRAVITY, FALLING
DOWN THE PIPES AND OUT OF THE BUILDING INTO THE SEWER.

    THE PIPING SYSTEM IN A BUILDING IS LIKE ARTERIES AND
VEINS RUNNING THROUGH A BODY. THE PIPES ARE CONNECTED TO
THE FIXTURES. ANOTHER SYSTEM OF PIPING INTRODUCES FRESH
AIR INTO THE PIPING TO PREVENT SIPHONING OF TRAPS, COM-
PRESSION, AND EXCESSIVE DETERIORATION DUE TO WASTE-WATER ACIDS.

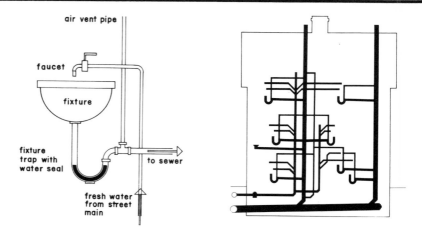

PLUMBING TRAPS PROVIDE A SEAL AGAINST ENTRANCE OF SEWER
GASES INTO THE BUILDING. A LITTLE WATER REMAINS IN THE BENT
PIPE WHEN THE FIXTURE IS DRAINED.

GRAVITY

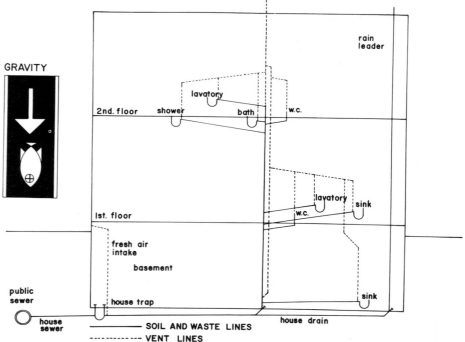

—————— SOIL AND WASTE LINES
------------ VENT LINES

### TYPICAL PLUMBING LAYOUT

74

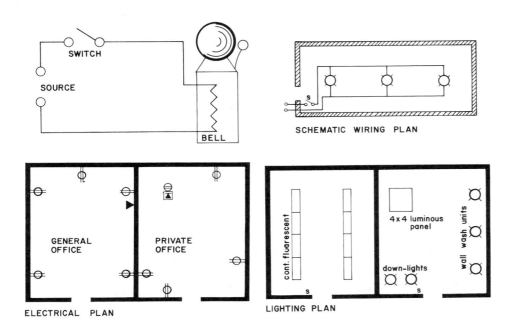

SWITCH

SOURCE

BELL

SCHEMATIC WIRING PLAN

GENERAL OFFICE     PRIVATE OFFICE

ELECTRICAL PLAN

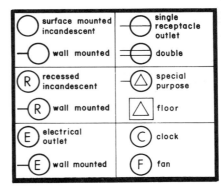

cont. fluorescent

4 x 4 luminous panel

wall wash units

down-lights

LIGHTING PLAN

THE DIFFERENCE IN POTENTIAL IS CALLED THE VOLT. THE AMPERE IS THE RATE OF CURRENT FLOW, AND THE WATT IS THE AMOUNT OF CURRENT CONSUMED. THE RATE AT WHICH ELECTRICAL ENERGY IS TRANSFORMED TO HEAT OR WORK IS CALLED ELECTRICAL POWER AND IS MEASURED IN WATTS.

THE ELECTRICAL BUILDING SYSTEMS ARE POWERED WITH TWO TYPES OF CURRENT, ALTERNATING (AC) AND DIRECT (DC). THE INTERIOR DESIGNER USUALLY USES ALTERNATING CURRENT. DIRECT CURRENT IS USED FOR LARGE MECHANICAL EQUIPMENT SUCH AS ELEVATORS AND EMERGENCY LIGHTING SYSTEMS.

ELECTRICAL POWER IS BROUGHT TO THE BUILDING BY THE ELECTRICAL COMPANY AND IS DISTRIBUTED THROUGH THE BUILDING BY THE DESIGNER. THE DISTRIBUTION CENTERS ARE PANEL BOXES WHICH TAKE THE POWER AND DIVIDE IT INTO CIRCUITS. ONE CIRCUIT WILL USUALLY HANDLE ABOUT 1,200 WATTS. LIGHTING IS USUALLY POWERED ON 1,10–1,20 VOLT CIRCUITS, AND EQUIPMENT SUCH AS STOVES, AIR CONDITIONERS, AND LARGER MOTORS IS POWERED ON 220 VOLT CIRCUITS. THE DESIGNER INDICATES WHERE THE CIRCUIT IS TO BE CONTROLLED FROM, THAT IS WHERE THE SWITCH IS TO BE PLACED, AND HOW MANY FIXTURES ARE TO BE ON EACH CIRCUIT.

THE OPERATION OF ELECTRICAL DEVICES SUCH AS LAMPS, HEATERS, MOTORS, AND RADIOS REQUIRES A CONTINUOUS FLOW OF ELECTRONS, IN OTHER WORDS AN ELECTRIC CURRENT. A COMPLETE PATH PROVIDED BY CONDUCTORS (WIRES) FOR THE ELECTRIC CURRENT IS AN ELECTRIC CIRCUIT. AN APPLIANCE SUCH AS A LAMP OR RADIO MUST BE CONNECTED IN A COMPLETE ELECTRICAL CIRCUIT. CURRENT FLOWS ONLY WHEN THE CIRCUIT IS COMPLETE.

IF THE CONDUCTING PATH OF THE CURRENT IS INTERRUPTED, THE FLOW OF CURRENT CEASES. THE ELECTRIC SWITCH IS USED TO COMPLETE OR OPEN AN ELECTRIC CIRCUIT. WHEN AN ELECTRIC LIGHT BULB BURNS OUT, THE CONDUCTING WIRE IN IT BREAKS AND OPENS THE CIRCUIT.

EVEN THOUGH AN ELECTRICAL CIRCUIT MAY BE COMPLETE, NO CURRENT WILL FLOW UNLESS A DIFFERENCE IN POTENTIAL IS PROVIDED. WATER WILL NOT FLOW IN A PIPE UNLESS THE PUMP MAINTAINS A STEADY DIFFERENCE IN PRESSURE SUFFICIENT TO PUSH THE WATER THROUGH THE PIPE. THE MECHANICAL ENERGY OF A GENERATOR IS USED TO MAINTAIN THE DIFFERENCE IN POTENTIAL IN AN ELECTRIC CIRCUIT.

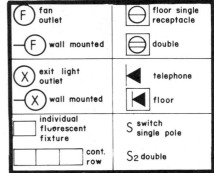

| | | | |
|---|---|---|---|
| surface mounted incandescent | single receptacle outlet | fan outlet | floor single receptacle |
| wall mounted | double | wall mounted | double |
| R recessed incandescent | special purpose | X exit light outlet | telephone |
| R wall mounted | floor | X wall mounted | floor |
| E electrical outlet | C clock | individual fluorescent fixture | S switch single pole |
| E wall mounted | F fan | cont. row | S2 double |

## HEAT MOVES FROM WARMER TO COOLER AREAS

**CONVECTION**-HEAT TRANSFERRED THROUGH ANOTHER MEDIUM: AIR, WATER, STEAM, GAS

**RADIATION**- HEAT RADIATED FROM HOT SURFACES IN A STRAIGHT LINE

**CONDUCTION**-HEAT TRAVELING THROUGH AN OBJECT SUCH AS A HOT IRON HELD IN A FIRE

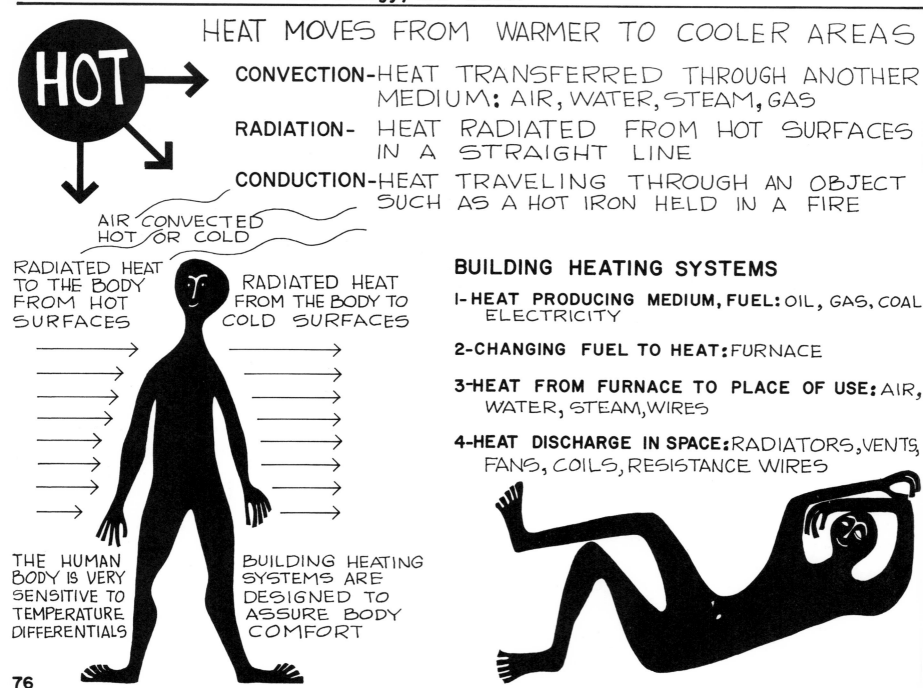

AIR CONVECTED HOT OR COLD

RADIATED HEAT TO THE BODY FROM HOT SURFACES

RADIATED HEAT FROM THE BODY TO COLD SURFACES

THE HUMAN BODY IS VERY SENSITIVE TO TEMPERATURE DIFFERENTIALS

BUILDING HEATING SYSTEMS ARE DESIGNED TO ASSURE BODY COMFORT

## BUILDING HEATING SYSTEMS

**1- HEAT PRODUCING MEDIUM, FUEL:** OIL, GAS, COAL, ELECTRICITY

**2- CHANGING FUEL TO HEAT:** FURNACE

**3- HEAT FROM FURNACE TO PLACE OF USE:** AIR, WATER, STEAM, WIRES

**4- HEAT DISCHARGE IN SPACE:** RADIATORS, VENTS, FANS, COILS, RESISTANCE WIRES

## HOT AIR HEATING

HOT AIR DISCHARGED INTO
ROOM BY FANS MIXES WITH
ROOM AIR.  AS AIR IS COOLED,
IT FALLS AND IS RETURNED
TO FURNACE FOR REHEATING
AND RECIRCULATION.

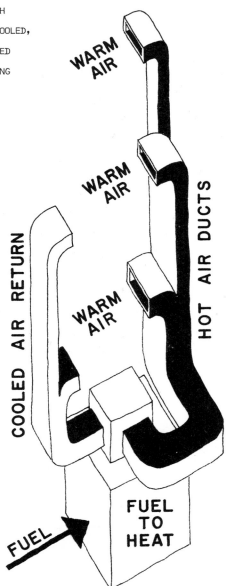

## HEATING  WITH STEAM

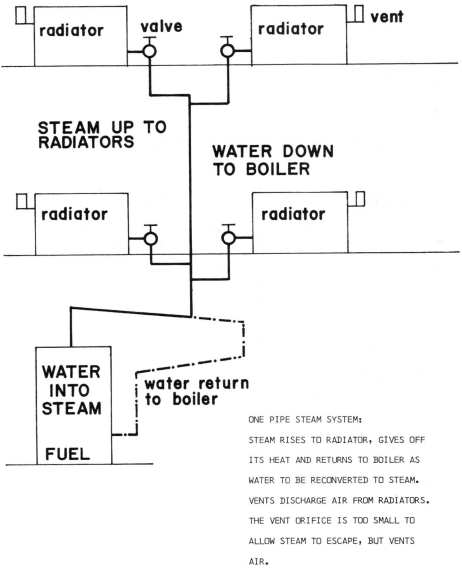

ONE PIPE STEAM SYSTEM:
STEAM RISES TO RADIATOR, GIVES OFF
ITS HEAT AND RETURNS TO BOILER AS
WATER TO BE RECONVERTED TO STEAM.
VENTS DISCHARGE AIR FROM RADIATORS.
THE VENT ORIFICE IS TOO SMALL TO
ALLOW STEAM TO ESCAPE, BUT VENTS
AIR.

# HEATING SYSTEMS

## HEATING WITH HOT WATER

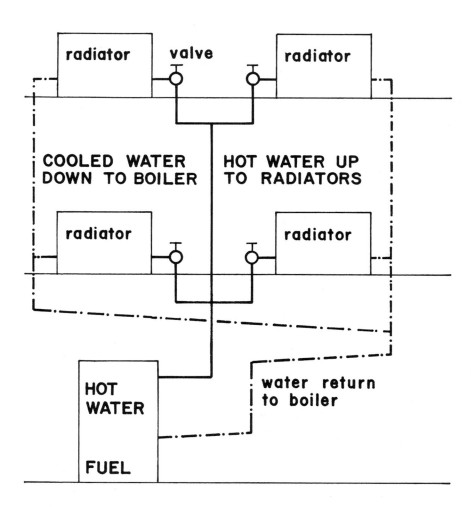

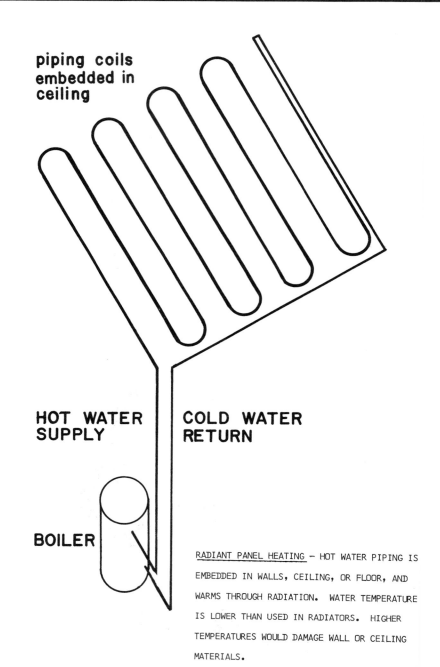

HOT WATER HEATING SYSTEM — HOT WATER IS FED DIRECTLY TO
RADIATORS AND IS RETURNED TO BOILER FOR REHEATING BY A
RETURN MAIN.   ROOM-HEAT DISCHARGE ELEMENTS MIGHT BE
BASEBOARD HEATING TUBES, RADIATORS, OR COILS WITH FANS
CIRCULATING AIR OVER THE HEATING COILS.

RADIANT PANEL HEATING — HOT WATER PIPING IS
EMBEDDED IN WALLS, CEILING, OR FLOOR, AND
WARMS THROUGH RADIATION.   WATER TEMPERATURE
IS LOWER THAN USED IN RADIATORS.   HIGHER
TEMPERATURES WOULD DAMAGE WALL OR CEILING
MATERIALS.

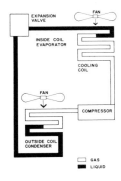

THE REFRIGERANT ABSORBS THE HEAT FROM THE AIR AT THE COOLING COIL AND THEN FLOWS TO THE COMPRESSOR, WHERE IT IS COMPRESSED AND DELIVERED TO THE CONDENSER. THERE IT DISCHARGES ITS HEAT. THE COOLED REFRIGERANT IS THEN RETURNED TO THE COOLING COIL, WHERE, IN THE ACT OF CHANGING BACK TO GAS, IT ABSORBS ROOM HEAT.

THE COMPRESSIVE REFRIGERATION CYCLE IS SIMPLY A WAY OF TRANSFERRING HEAT FROM ONE PLACE TO ANOTHER. THE MEANS FOR DOING THIS IS THE LIQUIFICATION AND EVAPORATION OF A REFRIGERANT, USUALLY FREON. DURING THE PROCESS, THE GAS ALTERNATELY GIVES OFF AND TAKES ON HEAT. HEAT IS EJECTED OUTSIDE OF THE COOLED AREA.

HEAT PUMPS USE THE REFRIGERATION CYCLE. IN COLD WEATHER THEY REVERSE AND BRING HEAT INTO THE SPACE THEY FORMERLY COOLED.

COOLING SYSTEMS, WHETHER CENTRAL OR WINDOW UNITS, OPERATE ON THE SAME PRINCIPLE. A FAN DRAWS AIR THROUGH A CLEANSING FILTER. THE AIR THEN PASSES OVER CHILLED COILS. MOISTURE IN THE AIR IS RELEASED (WARM AIR HOLDS MORE MOISTURE THAN COLD). A FAN THEN BLOWS THE COOLED AIR INTO LIVING SPACES EITHER THROUGH DUCTS IN A CENTRAL SYSTEM OR DIRECTLY THROUGH LOUVERS FROM WINDOW UNITS.

THE REFRIGERANT IS A LIQUID THAT BOILS AT A VERY LOW TEMPERATURE. AS ITS TEMPERATURE RISES TO THE BOILING POINT IT TURNS INTO GAS AND ABSORBS HEAT FROM THE SURROUNDING AIR. THE HEATED GAS IS THEN REMOVED TO THE OUT-SIDE, COMPRESSED, AND GIVES UP ITS HEAT AS IT RETURNS TO LIQUID. THE LIQUID THEN REPEATS THE CYCLE IN A CLOSED SYSTEM.

THE REFRIGERATING CYCLE USES THREE MAIN PIECES OF EQUIPMENT, THE COOLING COIL, THE COMPRESSOR, AND THE CONDENSER. THE COMPRESSOR ALSO PUMPS THE REFRIGERANT CONTINUOUSLY THROUGH THE CIRCUIT.

# CENTRAL AIR CONDITIONING

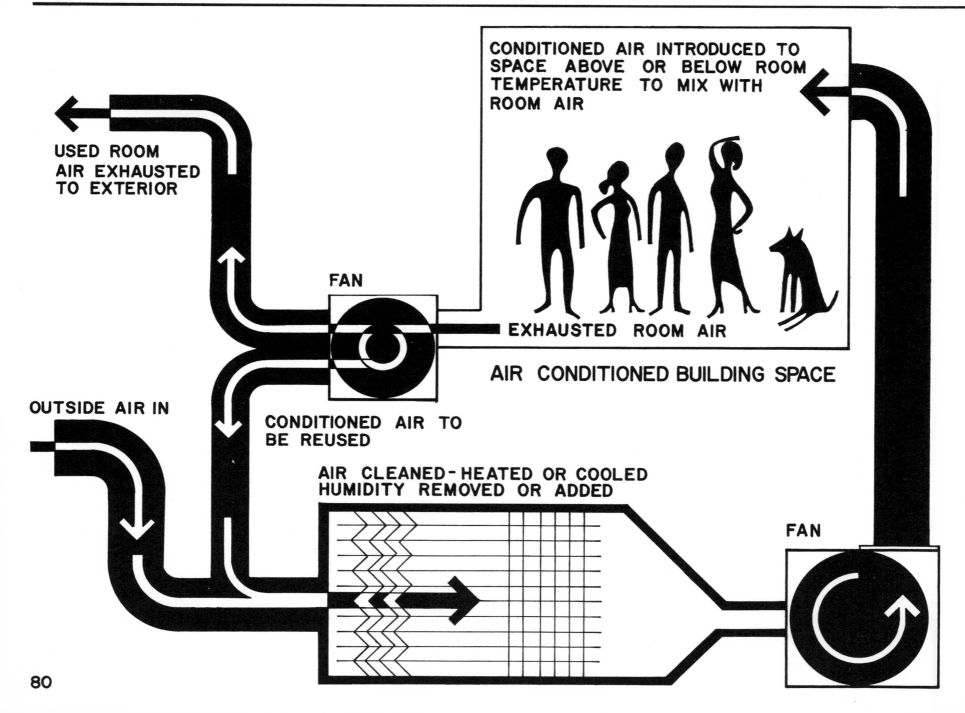

USED ROOM
AIR EXHAUSTED
TO EXTERIOR

CONDITIONED AIR INTRODUCED TO
SPACE ABOVE OR BELOW ROOM
TEMPERATURE TO MIX WITH
ROOM AIR

FAN

EXHAUSTED ROOM AIR

AIR CONDITIONED BUILDING SPACE

OUTSIDE AIR IN

CONDITIONED AIR TO
BE REUSED

AIR CLEANED-HEATED OR COOLED
HUMIDITY REMOVED OR ADDED

FAN

AIR CONDITIONING IS A SYSTEM OF YEAR-ROUND CLIMATE CONTROL, INCLUDING NOT ONLY SUMMER COOLING BUT WINTER HEATING, HUMIDITY CONTROL, AIR TURBULENCE, AND AIR CLEANING.

THE SIZE OF AIR CONDITIONING UNITS VARIES. THERE ARE THOSE THAT CAN BE PUT INTO A WINDOW AND DO NOTHING MORE THAN FILTER AND PUMP COOL AIR INTO THE ROOM. CENTRAL AIR CONDITIONING SYSTEMS COOL, TEMPER, HUMIDIFY, CLEANSE, AND MIX ROOM AIR WITH OUTSIDE AIR. GENERALLY SPEAK-ING, THE LARGER THE SYSTEM THE MORE AIR CONTROL IS EXERCISED.

THE INTERIOR DESIGNER SHOULD BE SURE THAT THERE ARE NO CRACKS THROUGH WHICH WARM AIR CAN ENTER THE SPACES. IT SHOULD BE REMEMBERED THAT LIGHTING AND PEOPLE HEAT SPACES. TOO LITTLE MOISTURE IN THE AIR WILL DRY THE MOIST MEMBRANES OF THE HUMAN BODY AND MAKE PEOPLE UNCOM-FORTABLE. TOO MUCH MOISTURE WILL NOT ALLOW THE BODY TO COOL ITSELF BY EVAPORATING MOISTURE THROUGH PERSPERATION.

THE MAJOR DECISIONS CONCERNING AIR CONDITIONING OF SPACES HAVE USUALLY BEEN MADE BY THE ARCHITECT AND ENGINEERS WHO HAVE SELECTED THE EQUIPMENT DURING THE DESIGN OF THE BUILDING. THE INTERIOR DESIGNER CAN ADJUST THESE DECISIONS BY THE USE OF WINDOW, WALL, AND FLOOR COVERINGS AND THE ADJUSTMENT OF AIR-FLOW PATTERNS AND AIR-CIRCULATION PATTERNS.

THESE CONDITIONS MUST BE ADJUSTED SO THAT THE OCCUPANTS OF A SPACE EXPERIENCE AN EQUILIBRIUM BETWEEN ACTIVITIES WHICH GENERATE BODILY HEAT AND THE INTERIOR TEMPERATURE CONDITIONS. HUMAN ACTIVITY AND ROOM AIR CONDITIONING FACTORS ARE INTERDEPENDENT.

THE INTERIOR CLIMATIC CONDITIONS MUST SUIT THE WIDE RANGE OF HUMAN PREFERENCE OF YOUNG AND OLD, ATHLETIC AND SEDENTARY, THOSE WHO LIKE IT HOT AND THOSE WHO LIKE IT COLD. FOR EXAMPLE, AIR AT A GIVEN TEMPERATURE WILL FEEL DIFFERENT IF ITS MOISTURE CONTENT IS HIGH OR LOW AND IF IT IS STILL OR TURBULENT. IT WILL FEEL DIFFERENT TO THOSE WHO HAVE JUST ENTERED THE ROOM AND TO THOSE WHO HAVE BEEN IN IT FOR SOME TIME.

SINCE IT IS OBVIOUSLY IMPOSSIBLE TO SATISFY EVERYONE, THE DESIGN SOLUTION IS TO FIND AN AVERAGE TEMPERATURE AND HUMIDITY LEVEL AND TO PREVENT DRAFTS AND VIOLENT CHANGES OF TEMPERATURE WITHIN THE SPACE.

HUMAN WELL-BEING DEPENDS UPON A NUMBER OF FACTORS SUCH AS PERCEPTUAL SATISFACTION, ACOUSTIC LEVEL, LIGHT LEVEL, AND THE FIVE FACTORS PROVIDED BY AIR CONDITIONING:

1 — TEMPERATURE OF SURROUNDING AIR

2 — RADIANT TEMPERATURE OF SURROUNDING SURFACES

3 — RELATIVE AIR HUMIDITY

4 — AIR MOTION

5 — CLEAN AIR WITHOUT DUST OR ODORS

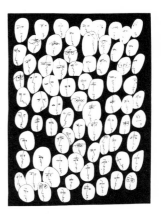

# THE SIZE OF PEOPLE

HUMAN SCALE IS THE SPACE IN WHICH THE OCCUPANT FEELS COMFORTABLE.  BUT COMFORT IS NOT THE ONLY CONSIDERATION.  HUMANS MUST HAVE ENOUGH SPACE IN WHICH TO MOVE AND PERFORM THEIR TASKS.  THE HUMAN BODY MUST HAVE CLEARANCE.  SOME OF THE SIZES ARE SHOWN HERE AND CAN BE FOUND IN ANY NUMBER OF BOOKS.  OF COURSE THEY ARE APPROXIMATE.  IF EVERYONE WERE THE SAME SIZE, HUMAN BEINGS COULD BE STAMPED OUT BY MACHINES.

THE SECOND DIMENSION IS HOW PEOPLE FEEL IN SPACE.  THIS IS THE AMOUNT OF SPACE WHICH MAKES THEM FEEL COMFORTABLE.  IT VARIES WITH CULTURES AND WITH EACH INDIVIDUAL HUMAN BEING.  DESIGNERS MUST USE ALL OF THEIR SKILL AND POWERS OF OBSERVATION TO HELP PEOPLE NOT ONLY HAVE THE SPACE THEY NEED TO MOVE, BUT ALSO THE SPACE IN WHICH THEY FEEL COMFORTABLE.

THINGS SUCH AS FURNITURE ARE ARRANGED FOR HUMAN COMFORT AND EASE OF MOVEMENT.  THE SIZE OF THE ROOM AND ITS ARCHITECTURAL ELEMENTS SUCH AS DOORS, WINDOWS, AND FIREPLACES ARE FIXED ELEMENTS.  THINGS HAVE SIZE.  THE NEGATIVE ROOM SPACE BETWEEN THE FIXED ARCHITECTURAL ELEMENTS AND THE ARRANGEABLE THINGS IS THE DESIGNER'S MATERIAL.

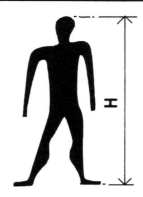

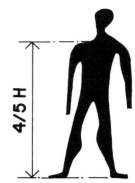

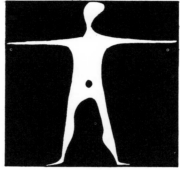

**SQUARE**

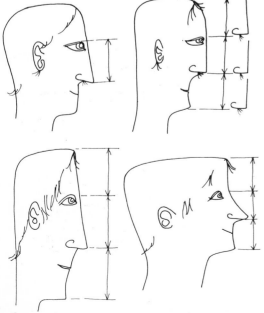

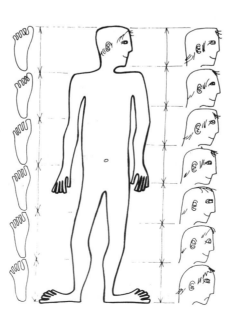

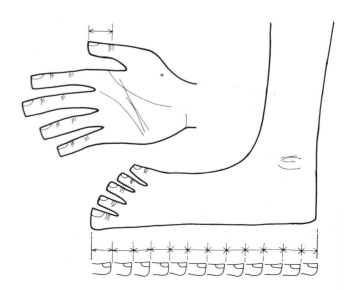

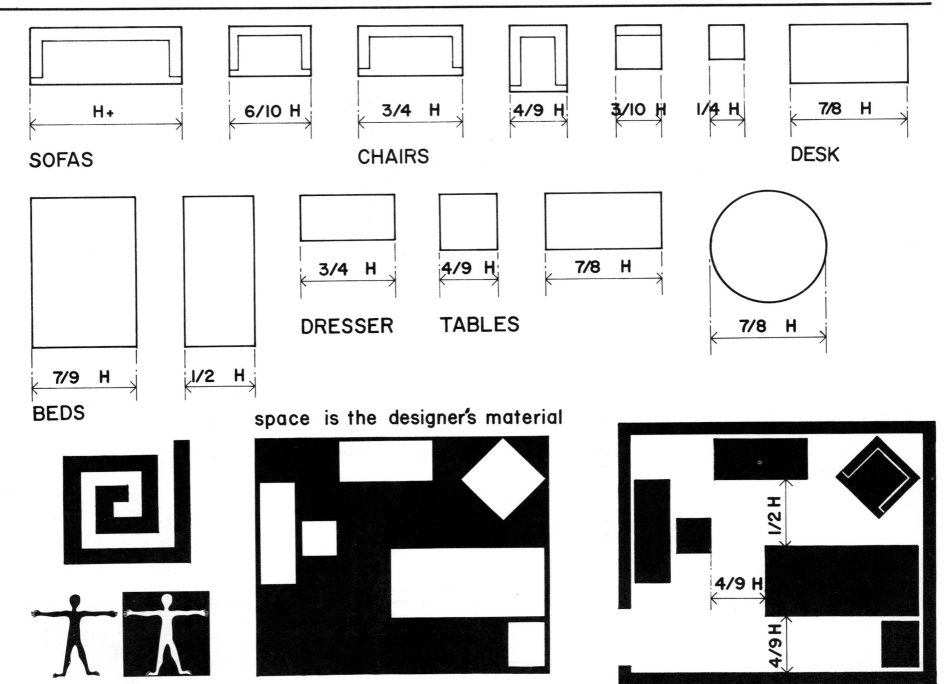

H+

SOFAS

6/10 H     3/4 H     4/9 H     3/10 H     1/4 H     7/8 H

CHAIRS                                          DESK

3/4 H     4/9 H     7/8 H     7/8 H

DRESSER     TABLES

7/9 H     1/2 H

BEDS

space is the designer's material

1/2 H     4/9 H     4/9 H

VISION IS A MIXTURE OF ILLUSION AND REALITY, BUT THERE ARE
VISUAL REACTIONS THAT CAN BE INTERPRETED AS GENERAL RULES.
IN SOME CASES THEY ARE OPTICAL ILLUSIONS, CONTRADICTIONS OF
THE VISUAL FACTS TRANSMITTED FROM THE EYE TO THE BRAIN.

PERCEPTUAL REACTIONS ARE EXTREMELY IMPORTANT TO THE
INTERIOR DESIGNER AS PART OF HIS COLLECTION OF WORKING TOOLS.
THE EXAMPLES SHOWN HERE ARE PRESENTED IN THE BINARY LANGUAGE
OF BLACK AND WHITE.  CONTRASTS ARE EASIER TO ISOLATE, DIS-
TINGUISH, AND IDENTIFY THAN THEY ARE IN THE THREE-DIMENSIONAL
WORLD OF INTERIOR DESIGN.

OPTICALLY, BLACK AND WHITE PRESENT THE EYE WITH EXTREMES
OF RETINAL STIMULATION.  THE EYE FLUCTUATES TO SUSTAIN A CON-
STANT IMAGE.  THE PROCESS OF ADAPTION MAY PRODUCE A SENSE OF
OVERLAPPING AND SHIFTING IMAGES.  THE SAME VISUAL EFFECTS
OCCUR SOMETIMES AMID THE PATTERNS, OBJECTS, AND ARCHITECTURAL
LINES IN THE DESIGN OF AN INTERIOR.

REMEMBER THERE IS NO ABSOLUTE QUALITY OF SIZE, SHAPE,
COLOR, BRIGHTNESS, LENGTH, OR WIDTH.  EVERY VISUAL UNIT IS
INFLUENCED BY ITS OPTICAL ENVIRONMENT AND THE RELATIONSHIPS
IT HAS WITH IT.  FOR EXAMPLE, TWO STRAIGHT PARALLEL LINES OF
EQUAL LENGTH SEEM DIFFERENT LENGTHS WHEN THEIR ENDINGS ARE
CHANGED, AND SEEM TO BEND WHEN PLACED ON A GRID OF RADIATING
LINES.

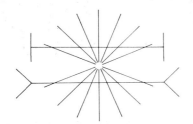

INTERRELATIONSHIPS CHANGE WITH CHANGES OF THE OPTICAL FIELD
(BACKGROUND).  THIS CAN BE DEMONSTRATED BY TURNING THE SHAPE
AROUND ITS CENTRAL AXIS, AND THEN CONTRASTING IT WITH THE
ORIGINAL.  WHICH OF THE TWO SQUARES IS LARGER, THE BLACK OR
THE WHITE.  THE WHITE APPEARS LARGER.  A BRIGHTLY ILLUMINATED
WHITE AREA IS THOUGHT TO PRODUCE AN IMAGE ON THE RETINA THAT
SPREADS OR AFFECTS THE RECEPTORS OF THE EYE IN A LESS
SELECTIVE WAY THAN A BLACK OR DARK GRAY IMAGE.

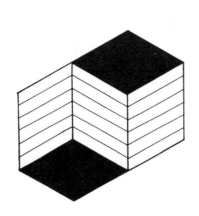

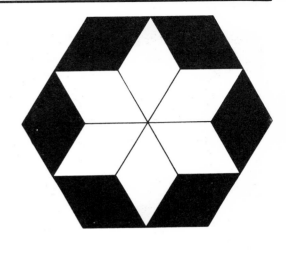

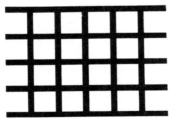

AS THE VIEWER STARES STEADILY AT THE HIGH CONTRAST BLACK-AND-WHITE
FIGURES, SMALL GRAY SPOTS BEGIN TO APPEAR IN THE INTERSECTIONS.

THE ABILITY TO DISTINGUISH AN OBJECT FROM ITS ENVIRONMENT BY SIZE,
SHAPE, VALUE, AND CLOSURE IS DETERMINED BY WHAT INFORMATION IS
PERCEIVED AS FIGURE AND WHAT AS GROUND.  THE FIGURE SEEMS TO EXIST IN
FRONT OF THE GROUND, WHICH IS SUBORDINATE.

SOMETIMES THIS RELATIONSHIP IS REVERSIBLE WHEN THE EYE CANNOT
CHOOSE BETWEEN THE POSITIVE AND NEGATIVE SHAPES AND IS FORCED TO
REPEATEDLY SHIFT FROM ONE AREA TO THE OTHER.

THE GREEK-KEY MOTIF, OR MEANDER, WITH INTERLOCKING BLACK-AND-
WHITE BANDS IS THE CLASSIC EXAMPLE OF THE REVERSIBLE FIGURE GROUND.

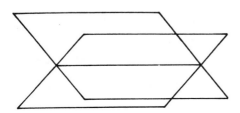

A VARIETY OF PERCEPTUAL EFFECTS CAN BE DEVELOPED WITHIN
A UNIFORM GEOMETRIC PATTERN.

IF THE INDIVIDUAL UNITS ARE SMALL ENOUGH OR ARE
VIEWED AT A DISTANCE THEY MAY FUSE TO PRODUCE A
SINGLE VALUE SUCH AS THE BLENDED TONES IN A NEWSPAPER
PHOTOGRAPH WHICH ARE CREATED ONLY WITH BLACK AND WHITE
DOTS.

WHEN THE UNITS ARE LARGE ENOUGH TO BE PERCEIVED
SEPARATELY THEY TEND TO CONNECT AND REGROUP ACCORDING
TO SHAPE AND FLUCTUATIONS OF THE VIEWER'S ATTENTION.
SYSTEMATIC VARIATION OF EITHER SHAPE, DIRECTION, SIZE,
NUMBER, OR VALUE RESULTS IN PULSATING, WARPING, AND
RELATED ILLUSIONS OF MOVEMENT. THE SCALE OF THE UNITS
AND THE VIEWING DISTANCE ARE IMPORTANT DETERMINANTS
OF THE EFFECT.

A WEIGHT OF LINE AND SPACING CAN GIVE THE ILLUSION OF
PERSPECTIVE. HEAVIER LINES APPEAR TO BE IN THE FOREGROUND.
THE LAWS OF PERSPECTIVE SAY THAT TO REPRESENT RECEDING
EQUAL ELEMENTS THEY MUST BECOME SUCCESSIVELY SMALLER AND
THE DISTANCE BETWEEN THEM MADE SMALLER.

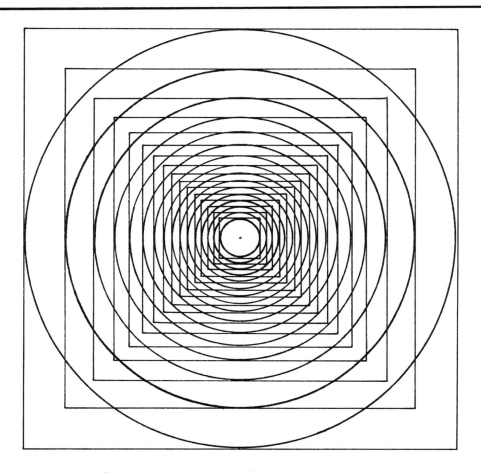

MOIRE IS THE TERM USED TO DESCRIBE THE OPTICAL ILLUSION THAT
EMERGES WHEN TWO OR MORE GEOMETRIC PATTERNS OVERLAP, AS CAN
BE OBSERVED IN THE ABOVE GRID OF OVERLAPPING CIRCLES AND
SQUARES.  THE EFFECT IS OFTEN FOUND IN REPETITIVE INDUSTRIAL
BUILDING ELEMENTS.

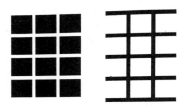

CLOSURE DESCRIBES THE PERCEPTUAL TENDENCY TO FILL IN GAPS OF
SPACES WHICH EXIST IN AN INCOMPLETE VISUAL PATTERN.  THE PRO-
TECTIVE COLORATION OF A ZEBRA OBSCURES VISUAL INFORMATION AND
EMBEDS THE ZEBRA'S FORM IN THE SURROUNDING GRASS AND TREES.
THE SAME EFFECT OCCURS WITH STRONG SHADOWS OR PATTERNS OF A
SPACE FRAME.

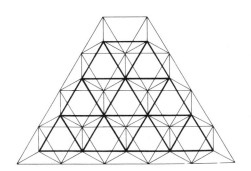

# PATTERNS OF STRUCTURE

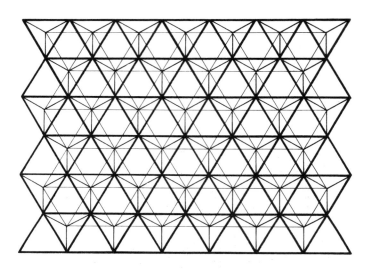

PATTERNS OF LIGHT AND SHADOW GENERATED BY STRUCTURAL FORM
IMPOSE A POWERFUL, OFTEN DOMINATING PATTERN ON INTERIOR
DESIGN.

THE EYE LEARNS TO ADJUST TO THE RIGHTNESS AND WRONGNESS OF
THE MESSAGES TRANSMITTED BY THE PATTERNS OF LIGHT AND SHADOW.
A SYMPATHETIC RELATIONSHIP SEEMS TO EXIST, IN WHICH HUMANS
CAN ALMOST FEEL THEMSELVES AS PART OF THE STRUCTURE.

A SPACE FRAME OF TRIANGULATED MEMBERS READS AS A FLAT PATTERN BUT IS
OBVIOUSLY STRUCTURAL. THE DOMINATING VISUAL ELEMENT IS THE MOIRE PATTERN
AT THE NODES, WHICH ARE THE POINTS OF STRUCTURAL INTERSECTION.

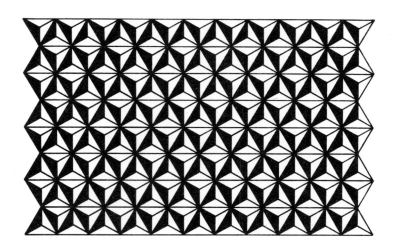

IN CONTRAST TO THE SPACE FRAME ABOVE THIS TRIANGULAR PATTERN COULD
EASILY BE PAPER, CLOTH, OR CLAY. THE MOIRE PATTERNS ARE DECORATIVE.

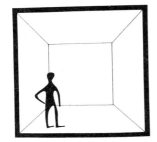

ALL STRUCTURES CONVEY MESSAGES. SPACE FRAMES AND SHELLS GIVE THE APPEARANCE OF TEXTURE SINCE THEY DISTRIBUTE FORCES IN A UNIFORM MANNER. SKELETAL STRUCTURES OF COLUMNS AND BEAMS, WHICH GATHER TOGETHER FORCES INTO ONE STRUCTURAL MEMBER AND CHANNEL THEM INTO THE FOUNDATION, ACCELERATE PERSPECTIVE.

THE HEIGHT AND STEEPNESS OF STAIRS TELL US SOMETHING ABOUT WHO THE DESIGNER THOUGHT WOULD USE THEM.

A SPACE WITHOUT STRUCTURAL HINTS IS AN UNINSPIRING SPACE.

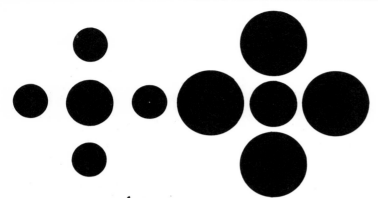

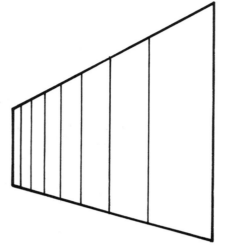

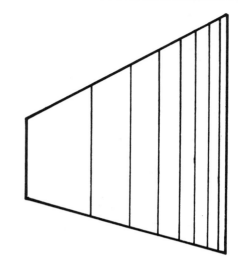

AN OBJECT'S ENVIRONMENT INFLUENCES ITS APPARENT SIZE —THE CENTER CIRCLES ARE IDENTICAL—

PARALLEL HORIZONTAL LINES SEEM TO CONVERGE AT EYE LEVEL. HORIZONTAL LINES SEEM TO DRAW CLOSER TOGETHER, AS AT LEFT. THE EFFECT CAN BE HEIGHTENED BY GRADUALLY REDUCING VERTICAL LINES, OR A SENSE OF CONFUSION CAN BE ENGENDERED BY VARYING VERTICAL LINES IN THE OPPOSITE DIRECTION, TOWARD THE OBSERVER, AS AT RIGHT.

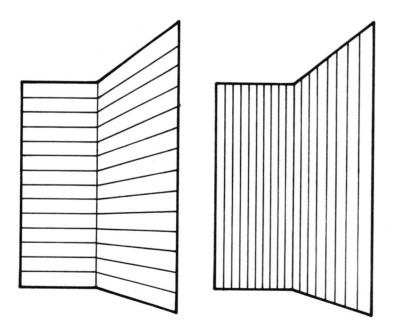

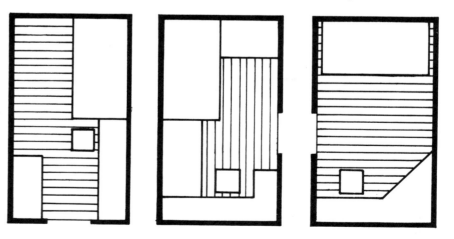

ROOMS WILL APPEAR STATIC OR DYNAMIC BY REPETITIONS OF WALL LINES. THEIR APPARENT DEPTH AND HEIGHT CHANGES AS WELL AS THE RATIO OF WALL TO FLOOR AND CEILING.

THE ARRANGEMENT OF DOORS, WINDOWS AND FURNITURE WILL CHANGE THE APPEARANCE OF A ROOM. FLOOR AND CEILING LINES CAN ALSO MAKE THE ROOM APPEAR LONGER OR SHORTER.

EVERY OBJECT IN THE ROOM BECOMES PART OF THE ROOM PATTERN. FIRST THERE ARE THE ARCHITECTURAL ELEMENTS SUCH AS THE ROOM SHAPE, DOORS, WINDOWS, ALCOVES, FIREPLACES, MOLDINGS, WINDOW DIVISIONS, AND DOOR PANELS. THEN THERE ARE THE PATTERNS OF THE FURNITURE LEGS, BACKS, SEATS, THE GRAIN OF WOOD PANELING, MASONRY JOINTS, ACOUSTIC CEILING TILE, BOOKS, PLANTS, AND ALL OF THE MISCEL-LANEOUS OBJECTS THAT PEOPLE SURROUND THEMSELVES WITH.

PATTERNS CAN UNIFY A ROOM AND GIVE IT CONSISTENCY OR CLASH IN A CONFUSION. PATTERNS CAN BE REPEATING OR NONREPEATING, IN SYMPATHY OR ANTAGONISTIC TO EACH OTHER.

A UNIQUE OBJECT SUCH AS A PLANT, SCULPTURE, OR PAINTING CAN GIVE A SPECIAL EMPHASIS TO A SPACE AND SUBDUE OR ELIMINATE OTHER PATTERNS.

INTERIOR DESIGN CAN BE THOUGHT OF AS THE ARRANGEMENT OF PATTERNS.

# TEXTURE

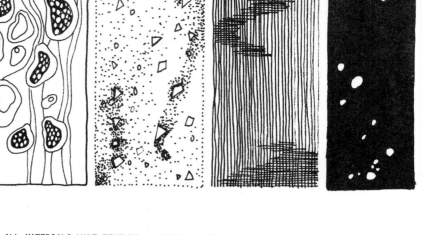

ALL MATERIALS HAVE TEXTURE. TEXTURAL QUALITIES GIVE PHYSICAL REACTIONS WHEN TOUCHED. SOME PEOPLE SHIVER WHEN THEY PICK UP A BRICK OR HANDLE A PEACH. WE HAVE TACTILE REACTION TO MATERIALS EVEN THOUGH WE DO NOT TOUCH THEM. SOME MATERIALS SEEM GOOD TO HANDLE AND OTHERS NOT. A COMPOSITION OF TEXTURES CAN HAVE THE SAME EFFECT ON US AS THE COMPOSITION OF COLORS. TEXTURES CAN ACCENTUATE SHAPE OR POSITION IN SPACE, GIVE THE IMPRESSION OF NEARNESS OR DISTANCE, AND UNIFY OR DESTROY THE DESIGN OF A ROOM.

MATERIAL SURFACES TRANSMIT SIGNALS TO THE BRAIN THROUGH THE EYE. WE DETERMINE WHETHER THEY ARE SOFT OR HARD, BRITTLE OR RESILIENT, AND BLEND THIS INTERPRETATION INTO THEIR FEELING WHEN WE TOUCH THEM.

CERTAIN TEXTURES SEEM TO HARMONIZE AS CERTAIN COLORS DO. THE COMBINATION OF TEXTURES IS THEREFORE AS IMPORTANT AS THE COMBINATION OF COLORS.

WE BRING THE RANGE OF ASSOCIATION WE HAVE GAINED FROM NATURAL MATERIALS TO THE NEW MATERIALS SUCH AS PLASTICS. AT FIRST THEY WERE THOUGHT TO BE ONLY CHEAP IMITATIONS, BUT THIS NO LONGER HOLDS TRUE. SYNTHETIC MATERIALS HAVE BROUGHT AN ENTIRELY NEW RANGE OF COLOR AND TEXTURE INTO INTERIORS, THUS ENLARGING THE DESIGNER'S RANGE OF CHOICE.

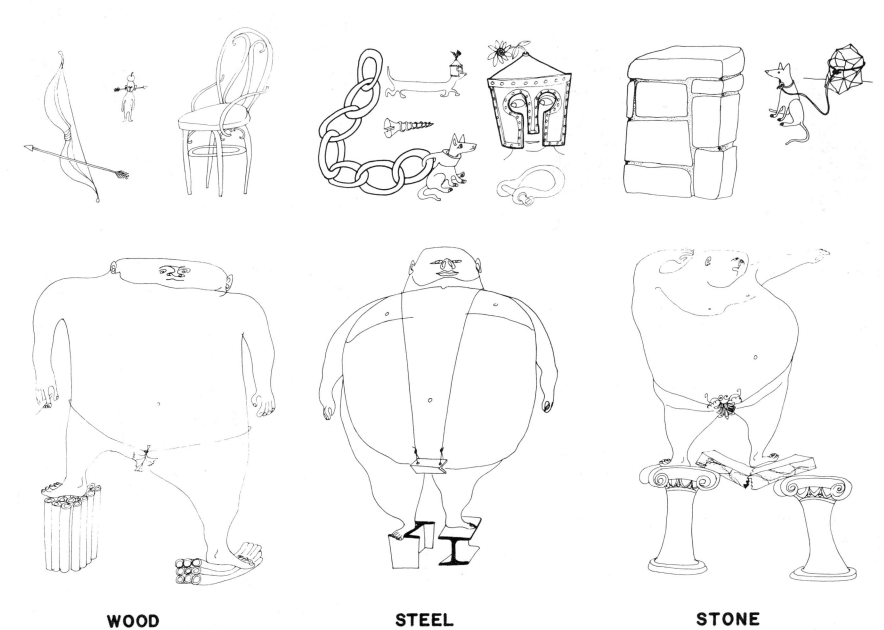

**WOOD**          **STEEL**          **STONE**

# ORDER

## random rounds

## squared circles

## TETRAHEDRON

## CUBE

### obvious order

THE HUMAN REACTION TO SIMPLE ABSTRACT GEOMETRIC FORMS IS UNEMOTIONAL.  A
TETRAHEDRON IS OBVIOUSLY COMPOSED OF FOUR EQUILATERAL TRIANGLES, A CUBE
OF SIX SQUARES.

THE ABSTRACT FORMS OF NATURE REPRESENT COMPLEX, OFTEN INCOMPREHENSIBLE
ORDERS.  WE SEEK MEANING IN THEM BY ASSOCIATION WITH HUMAN ATTRIBUTES.  A
FIR TREE IS PROUD, AN OAK POWERFUL, A WILLOW SAD, A ROCK STRONG, AND A
MOUNTAIN NOBLE.

DESIGN IS A MEANS OF INTRODUCING ORDER INTO THE ENVIRONMENT.  THE
DESIGNER WALKS A TIGHROPE BETWEEN THE ORDERS THAT ARE RATIONALLY COMPREHENDED
AND THOSE THAT ARE INSTINCTIVELY FELT.

## FRETS

### rhythmic order

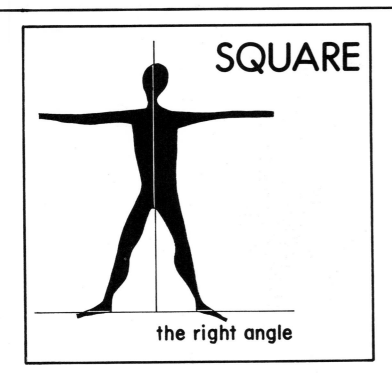

# SQUARE

### the right angle

## THE 'RIGHT' RIGHT ANGLE AND THE SQUARE

THE RIGHT ANGLE IS A UNIVERSALLY ACCEPTED FACT OF DESIGN.
WE STAND VERTICALLY UPON THE EARTH. WATER, OR ANY OTHER
SUBSTANCE THAT HAS THE CHANCE, WILL RECLINE PARALLEL TO
THE EARTH'S SURFACE. THE ANGLE BETWEEN THE VERTICAL AND
THE HORIZONTAL IS 90 DEGREES, A RIGHT ANGLE, AND 4 RIGHT
ANGLES COMBINED WITH 4 EQUAL SIDES MAKE A SQUARE, A
PLEASING, USEFUL, AND, ACCORDING TO THE ANCIENTS, A
MYSTICAL FIGURE. WE USE THE RIGHT ANGLE BECAUSE IT IS
GOOD FOR BUILDING AND LOOKS "RIGHT".

# BALANCE

PHYSICAL AND PERCEPTUAL BALANCE SEEM INSTINCTIVE. TWO CHILDREN ON A SEESAW
QUICKLY FIND A BALANCE BETWEEN THEIR WEIGHT AND THE DISTANCE FROM THE CENTER.
OUR EYE INSTINCTIVELY SEEKS THE CENTER OF OBJECTS. THERE ARE INNUMERABLE
PHYSICAL AND PERCEPTUAL BALANCES THAT CAN BE ACHIEVED, BUT THEY CAN ALL BE
DIVIDED INTO TWO CATEGORIES: 1. THE BALANCE ACHIEVED BY IDENTICALS AND
2. THE BALANCE OF DIFFERENCES COMBINED TO CREATE EQUALITIES.

**EQUAL**                                                      **EQUAL**

**CENTER**

## MORE EQUAL                          LESS EQUAL

**OFF** **CENTER**

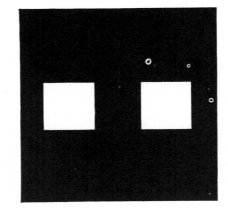

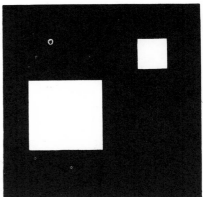

# COLOR

# COLOR

COLOR IS SAID TO INDUCE A SENSE OF WELL—BEING, DISCOMFORT, ACTIVITY, OR PASSIVITY. IT HAS INFLUENCE IN ENLARGING OR DIMINISHING THE APPARENT SIZE AND DIMENSION OF ROOMS AND IN CREATING ROOM ATMOSPHERE.

IT IS CERTAIN THAT COLOR EXERTS AN INFLUENCE UPON ROOM OCCUPANTS. IT IS NOT AS CERTAIN THAT THESE EFFECTS CAN BE PREDICTED WITH ABSOLUTE CERTAINTY.

THE FOLLOWING OBSERVATIONS ARE TO BE USED AS GUIDES FOR THE INTERIOR DESIGNER AND CONFIRMED BY EXPERIENCE AND OBSERVATION.

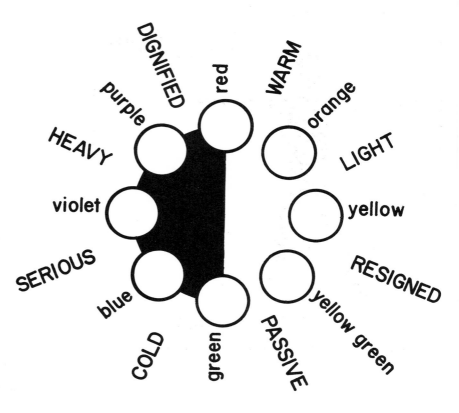

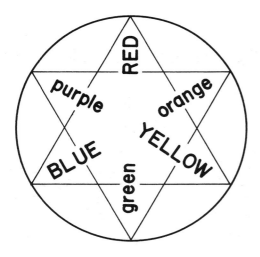

COLOR CIRCLE—MAJOR TRIANGLE OF RED, BLUE, YELLOW, WHICH ARE PRIMARY COLORS, AND OPPOSED TRIANGLE OF GREEN, ORANGE, PURPLE, WHICH ARE SECONDARY COLORS RESULTING FROM THE MIXING OF PRIMARY COLORS.

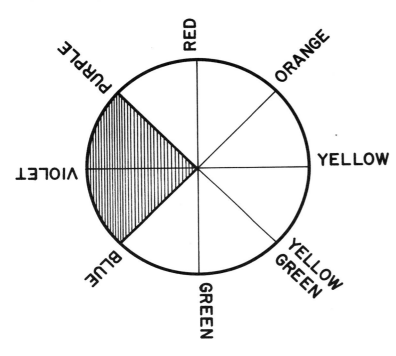

THE DISTRIBUTION OF RED WITHIN A COLOR GIVES
IT A SENSATION OF WEIGHT.

A COLOR WHEEL OF TWELVE COLORS

ORANGE IS SAID TO BE THE MOST VIGOROUS COLOR, FOLLOWED BY YELLOW, RED, GREEN, AND PURPLE. BLUE, BLUE-GREEN, AND VIOLET ARE CONSIDERED TO BE COLD, PASSIVE, AND THE LEAST FORCEFUL.

VIGOROUS COLORS, IT IS SAID, ARE BEST USED IN SMALL AREAS AND THE MORE PASSIVE COLORS IN LARGE SPACES. THE EFFECT OF COLOR DEPENDS ON ITS BRIGHTNESS AND POSITION.

IT IS THOUGHT THAT WARM, LIGHT COLORS ARE PSYCHOLOGICALLY STIMU-LATING WHEN PLACED ABOVE, GIVE AN IMPRESSION OF WARMTH FROM THE SIDE, AND HAVE AN ELEVATING EFFECT WHEN PLACED LOW IN THE ROOM.

WARM, DARK COLORS PLACED HIGH IN A ROOM ARE DIGNIFIED. FROM THE SIDE THEY ARE SAID TO BE LIMITING AND ENCLOSING, AND PLACED LOW IN THE ROOM GIVE A SENSE OF SECURITY.

COLD, LIGHT COLORS ABOVE ARE RELAXING, WHILE FROM THE SIDE THEY SUGGEST SPACIOUSNESS AND FROM BELOW GIVE THE APPEARANCE OF BEING SMOOTH TO WALK ON.

COLD, DARK COLORS ARE THREATENING ABOVE, TEND TO BE DEPRESSING FROM THE SIDE, AND IMPART A FEELING OF LABORIOUS EFFORT IF USED BELOW.

WHITE IMPLIES PURITY, CLEANLINESS, AND ORDER. IT PLAYS AN IMPORTANT PART IN SEPARATING COLOR ARRANGEMENTS AND NEUTRALIZING AND THUS ANIMATING AND ARTICULATING THE SCHEME.

# COLOR AND LIGHT

SUCCESSFUL COLOR SCHEMES CANNOT BE SPECIFIED. COLOR CANNOT BE DESCRIBED IN WORDS. IT MUST BE DEMONSTRATED IN PAINT AND MATERIAL SAMPLES AND IN THE COLOR OF LIGHT.

THE IMPORTANT FACT TO UNDERSTAND WHEN WORKING WITH COLOR IS THE RELATIONSHIP BETWEEN THE COLOR RAYS OF THE SPECTRUM AND THE PIGMENTS OF MATERIALS.

DAYLIGHT AND ALL WHITE LIGHT IS COMPOSED OF A GRADUATION OF BRIGHTLY COLORED RAYS, RANGING FROM RED TO VIOLET. THE SPECTRUM IS APPARENT IN A RAINBOW OR WHEN LIGHT PASSES THROUGH A PRISM. THIS IS THE RANGE OF COLOR WITH WHICH THE INTERIOR DESIGNER WORKS. PAINTS AND DYES ARE SIMPLY THE MEANS OF ABSORBING CERTAIN BANDS OF LIGHT AND REFLECTING OTHERS. IN ARTIFICIAL LIGHT, COLOR EFFECTS ARE LIMITED BY THE RANGE OF LIGHT USED. IF THE LIGHT LACKS BLUES, THE BLUES IN THE SCHEME WILL SUFFER. IF THE LIGHT USED IS RED, THE EFFECT WILL BE DINGY FOR THERE WILL BE NO CONTRASTS FROM THE REFLECTED LIGHT OF OTHER COLORS.

THE DESIGNER MUST THINK IN TERMS OF SPECTRAL COLORS, WHETHER THEY ARE IN THE DAYLIGHT SPECTRUM OR IN THE SLIGHTLY DIFFERENT RANGE OF ARTIFICIAL LIGHT, RATHER THAN IN TERMS OF PIGMENTS AND DYES. PAINT IS ONLY A MEANS OF CONTROLLING THE TRUE SOURCE OF COLOR, WHICH IS ALWAYS LIGHT.

A COLORED SURFACE HAS ABSORBED LIGHT FROM THAT PART OF THE SPECTRUM THAT IT DOES NOT REFLECT. A RED WALL ABSORBS MOST OF THE BLUE AND GREEN LIGHT THAT FALLS ON IT. A BLUE RUG WILL ABSORB THE REDS.

IT IS SELDOM TAKEN INTO CONSIDERATION THAT A STRONGLY COLORED INTERIOR WILL ABSORB HALF THE LIGHT THAT FALLS UPON ITS SURFACES. THIS MEANS A SERIOUS LOSS OF LUMENS AND EXPENSIVE WATTAGE. EVERY STRONG COLOR IN AN INTERIOR IS PAID FOR IN TERMS OF RADIANT ENERGY. THE PROBLEM IS HOW TO KEEP ENOUGH LIGHT REFLECTING AROUND THE SURFACES OF AN INTERIOR WITHOUT PRODUCING AN INSIPID COLOR SCHEME.

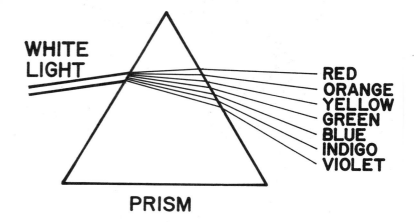

**WHITE LIGHT** → **PRISM** → **RED ORANGE YELLOW GREEN BLUE INDIGO VIOLET**

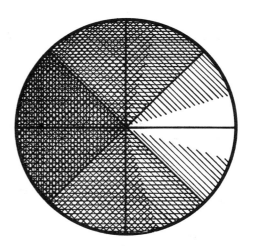

the color wheel
and absorption of
radiant energy

WITH BLACK-AND-WHITE OBJECTS OF THE
SAME SIZE, THE WHITE APPEARS LARGER.

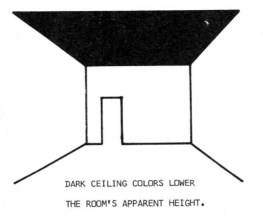

DARK CEILING COLORS LOWER
THE ROOM'S APPARENT HEIGHT.

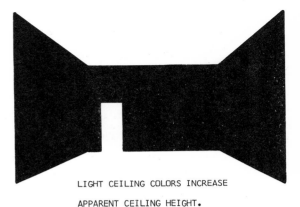

LIGHT CEILING COLORS INCREASE
APPARENT CEILING HEIGHT.

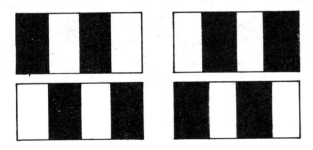

TO MAKE DARK AND LIGHT AREAS APPEAR THE SAME
SIZE, REDUCE THE SIZE OF LIGHT AREAS.

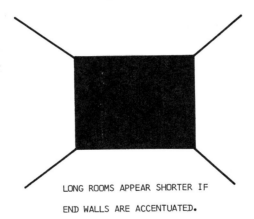

LONG ROOMS APPEAR SHORTER IF
END WALLS ARE ACCENTUATED.

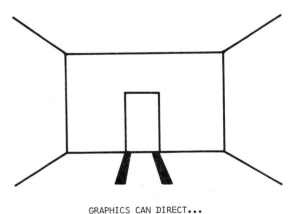

GRAPHICS CAN DIRECT...

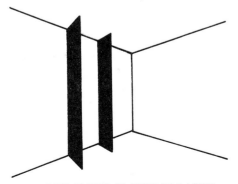

DARK OBJECTS IN FRONT OF A LIGHT
WALL ARE EMPHASIZED.

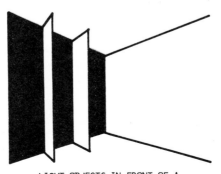

LIGHT OBJECTS IN FRONT OF A
DARK WALL ARE LESS PRONOUNCED.

OR DESTROY SPACE GEOMETRY.

# EMPHASIS AND DIRT

IF SPACES ARE TO BE EMPHASIZED AND UNIFIED THE FLOOR OR CEILING SHOULD
BE MADE A STRONG COLOR.  IF THE DESIRE IS TO EMPHASIZE AN ISOLATED AREA,
CHANGE THE COLOR OF THE WALLS AND FLOOR.

WALL HANGINGS WILL BE IMMENSELY MORE EFFECTIVE IF THE WALL BEHIND
THEM IS COMPLEMENTARY IN A STRONG OR CLEAR COLOR.

THE LOGIC OF COLOR CAN BE USED TO CONTRADICT THE LOGIC OF FORM.
BUT JOKES IN DESIGN SHOULD BE USED SPARINGLY.

NONDESCRIPT ROOMS IN PLAN AND FURNITURE CAN BE GIVEN CHARACTER AND
WARMTH AND EVEN SCALE WITH AN INTELLIGENT USE OF COLOR.

INSIGNIFICANT ARCHITECTURAL DETAILS AND UNTIDY OBJECTS CAN BE CAMOU-
FLAGED WITH COLOR AND PATTERNS.  THIS IS AN APPROPRIATE USE FOR THE STRONG
RICH COLORS.  THEY SET A KEY THAT MINIMIZES DETAILS.  DARK GREENS, FOR
EXAMPLE, CAN CONCEAL WORN BOOK COVERS, BUT DARK GREENS, BURNT ORANGES, AND
SUBTLE KHAKIS ALSO ABSORB A GREAT MANY LUMENS.

THE ALTERNATIVES MUST BE WEIGHED BEFORE THE DECISION IS MADE AND THE
BRUSH APPLIED.

A FUNDAMENTAL PROBLEM OF INTERIOR DESIGN IS DIRT AND WEAR.  THERE ARE
A NUMBER OF APPROACHES TO THE PROBLEM.  FIRST, THERE IS THE PROTECTIVE
COLORING SCHOOL WHICH HOLDS THAT THE NEARER THE COLOR OF A ROOM IS TO THE
COLOR OF DIRT THE LESS THE DIRT WILL SHOW.  THE RESULTS ARE DIRTCOLORED
COLORS, WHICH MAKE THE ROOM LOOK DIRTY BEFORE IT GETS DIRTY.

THE REVERSE POSITION ADVOCATES USING THE CLEANEST, LIGHTEST COLORS
POSSIBLE.  THE SPACE APPEARS DAZZLINGLY CLEAN, AND THE RESPONSIBILITY OF
KEEPING IT SO RESTS ON THE OCCUPANTS.

A THIRD APPROACH IS TO CAMOUFLAGE DIRT.  THIS TECHNIQUE CAN BE USED TO
CONCEAL SUCH MARKS AS FOOTPRINTS ON A FLOOR.  A STRONG PATTERN IN BLACK
AND WHITE MAKES IT ALMOST IMPOSSIBLE FOR THE EYE TO DISTINGUISH PALER
SURFACE MARKS.  EVEN WHEN THE DESIGNER DOES NOT WISH TO USE THIS TECHNIQUE,
HE MIGHT STRIVE TO MAKE THE INTERIOR SO INTERESTING THAT DUST AND STAINS
GO UNNOTICED.

THE FOURTH APPROACH IS TO LET THE STRUCTURAL MATERIALS OF THE BUILDING
SERVE AS DECORATIVE SURFACES.  BRICK, WOOD, AND TILES HAVE TEXTURES, COLORS,
AND VARIATIONS OF THEIR OWN WHEN THEY ARE NOT COVERED WITH PLASTER AND PAINT.
ARCHITECTURAL MATERIALS SUCH AS THESE MAY CATCH AND HOLD DIRT IN MORTAR JOINTS,
BUT THEY WILL STAND MORE AND HEAVIER CLEANING.  THE DESIGNER HAS TO SPECIFY
THESE MATERIALS AT THE BEGINNING OF THE PROJECT, WHEN THE BUILDING IS UNDER
CONSTRUCTION; OTHERWISE THEY BECOME PROHIBITIVELY EXPENSIVE.

INVARIABLY THERE ARE A NUMBER OF FIXED COLORS AND TEXTURES IN EXISTING FURNITURE, ORNAMENTS, BOOKS, WOOD, MARBLE, TERAZZO, AND TILE WHICH MUST BE CONSIDERED.

SELECTED LIGHT FIXTURES, HARDWARE, AND HEATING GRILLS MUST ALSO BE CONSIDERED WHEN THE COLOR SCHEME IS PLANNED. EVERY OBJECT HAS COLOR AND TEXTURE WHICH WILL CONTRIBUTE TO THE DESIGN SCHEME.

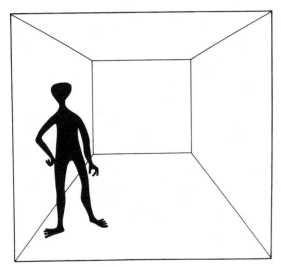

IF MANUFACTURED ITEMS ARE CHOSEN FIRST AND PAINTS AND WALL COVERINGS SELECTED AFTER AND MATCHED TO THEM, COLOR COORDINATION IS EASIER THAN STARTING WITH A BACKGROUND COLOR AND THEN SEARCHING FOR COLORS AND TEXTURES TO CONFORM. IT IS COMPARATIVELY EASY TO MATCH PAINT TO A DIFFICULT CARPET COLOR, BUT QUITE HARD TO FIND THE RIGHT COLOR IN MASS-PRODUCED MANUFACTURED ITEMS TO MATCH PAINT.

A LARGE PROPORTION OF THE SURFACE AREA IN ANY INTERIOR IS TAKEN UP BY THE FLOOR. THIS IS A MAJOR ELEMENT IN THE COLOR SCHEME. IF THE FLOOR IS OF FINE MATERIAL SUCH AS HARDWOOD OR TILE IT MAY DOMINATE THE SCHEME.

THE RELATION BETWEEN THE WALL AND THE FLOOR SURFACES AS THEY MEET AT RIGHT ANGLES IS ONE OF THE MAJOR DESIGN EFFECTS. AS THE SCALE OF THE INTERIOR BECOMES MORE MODEST, SO THE SCOPE FOR BROAD EFFECTS BECOMES LESS. THIS IS THE REASON THAT THE RELATION OF WALLS TO FLOOR CANNOT BE OVEREMPHASIZED. IT PROVIDES THE SMALL HOUSEHOLD DECORATOR WITH A MAJOR OPPORTUNITY TO CREATE AN EFFECT.

THE STRONGER THE WALL COLORS, THE LESS LIGHT WILL BE REFLECTED. THE SENSIBLE DESIGNER WILL DETERMINE HOW IMPORTANT THE ROOM SURFACES ARE FOR REFLECTION BEFORE CONSIDERING THE COLOR SCHEME. IN A WHITE ROOM, THE FLOOR AND ITS RELATION TO THE FURNITURE AND THE VARIOUS ORNAMENTS IS A PRIMARY CONCERN.

WHITE WALLS AND CEILINGS SIMPLIFY MIXING OF ROOM COLORS. THE WHITE ROOM HAS ONE MAJOR DESIGN ASSET. THE PRESENCE OF WHITE AND THE HIGH LEVEL OF REFLECTION GIVE THE DESIGNER THE WIDEST POSSIBLE RANGE BETWEEN THOSE LIGHT AND DARK CONTRASTS WHICH GIVE A ROOM MUCH OF ITS VITALITY.

WHETHER THE COLOR IS USED FOR PLEASURE OR FOR DEFINITE PURPOSE SUCH AS REDUCING OR INCREASING SCALE, IT IS IMPORTANT THAT COLOR EMPHASIZES THE PLAN AND FORM OF THE INTERIOR.

BRIGHT SPOTS AND STRONG CONTRASTS ATTRACT THE EYE. THIS ATTRACTION MUST OCCUR AT POINTS THE DESIGNER WANTS PEOPLE TO LOOK AT.

TO MAP OUT IN THE
MIND ● TO PLAN PROJECT●
INVENT●TO DRAW●TO
DESCRIBE ●SKETCH IN OUTLINE
AS A CONCEPTION OR A
PLAN● TO PROPOSE ●INTEND
●TO PLAN OR CONTRIVE
FOR A PURPOSE●TO INDICATE
●TO SCHEME

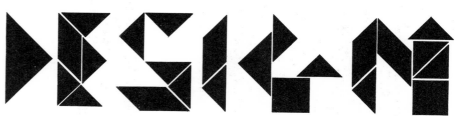

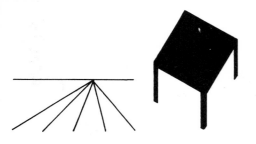

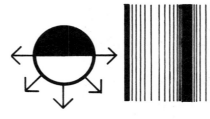

SPACE   STRUCTURE   MATERIALS   LIGHT   SOUND   PUZZLE

ELEMENTS OF INTERIOR DESIGN

PIECES OF A PUZZLE

# HOW DO THEY GO TOGETHER?

SINCE DESIGN IS LIKE A PUZZLE
WE CAN USE A PUZZLE TO
EXPLAIN DESIGN

## TANGRAM

A SQUARE IS CUT
INTO SEVEN PIECES

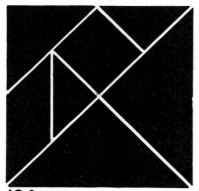

**THE RULES ARE:**

● ALL SEVEN PIECES
MUST BE USED

● PIECES MUST
TOUCH BUT CAN
NOT OVERLAP

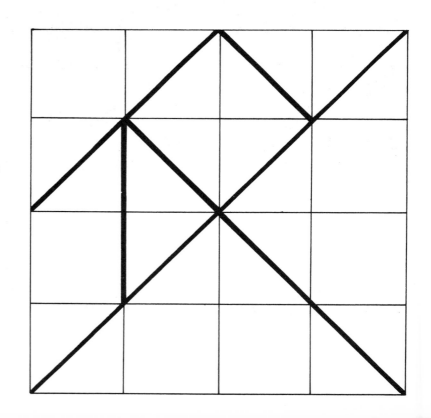

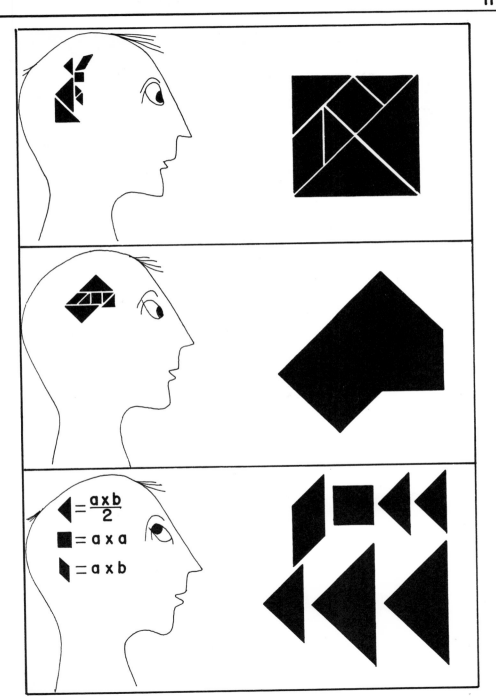

TO DESIGN IS TO PLAN, USING INTUITION, EXPERIENCE, AND ANALYSIS. WE TAKE THINGS APART TO SEE HOW THEY WORK AND ONCE WE UNDERSTAND THE PARTS, REASSEMBLE THEM INTO NEW COMBINATIONS. WE CAN LOOK AT OTHER THINGS AND UNDERSTAND HOW THEY ARE PUT TOGETHER FROM THIS EXPERIENCE. THIRDLY WE CAN SEEK UNIVERSAL QUALITIES OF THE PARTS THAT HELP US MAKE DECISIONS, INVENT NEW FORMS, AND UNDERSTAND HOW THINGS ARE PUT TOGETHER.

THE TANS (PIECES OF THE PUZZLE) CAN BE USED TO MAKE ABSTRACT FIGURES OF PEOPLE, ANIMALS OR INANIMATE OBJECTS TO CONVEY A MESSAGE. THIS IS ANALOGOUS TO ARRANGING THE PARTS OF AN INTERIOR TO EXPRESS A MOOD OR FEELING— INTIMACY, DIGNITY, RELAXATION.

THE SECOND WAY OF USING THE TANS IS TO EXPLORE THE POSSIBILITY OF COM— POSING A PARTICULAR GEOMETRIC CONFIGURATION WITH THE SEVEN PIECES OF THE PUZZLE. THIS IS LIKE FITTING THE PARTS OF A DESIGN INTO A GIVEN SPACE.

THE THIRD USE OF THE PUZZLE PIECES IS DESIGN RESEARCH. WE SEEK OUT THE UNIVERSAL CHARACTERISTICS OF THE ELEMENTS AND FROM THESE ABSTRACT GENERAL PRINCIPLES. FOR EXAMPLE, WE FIND THAT OF ALL THE GIVEN FIGURES THE ONE THAT ENCLOSES MOST AREA WITH THE LEAST PERIMETER LENGTH IS A SQUARE.

IN ALL THREE USES INTUITION, EXPERIENCE, AND, ANALYSIS PLAY A PART. INTUITION WOULD BE THE MOST IMPORTANT IN THE FIRST APPROACH, EXPERIENCE IN THE SECOND, AND ANALYSIS IN THE THIRD, BUT SOME OF EACH IS USED AT EACH STAGE IN SEEKING AND FINDING THE SOLUTIONS TO ALL PUZZLES AND DESIGN PROBLEMS.

Bubble diagrams are like tangram-simply a game of arranging parts

bubble **WHAT IT IS** connection

THE BUBBLE MAKES PART OF THE PROBLEM VISIBLE. THE CONNECTION SHOWS RELATIONSHIP BETWEEN THE PARTS.

## PARTS OF THE BUBBLE PUZZLE

LIVING' ROOM (L.R.)
LIBRARY (LIB.)
DINING ROOM (D.R.)
BEDROOM I (B.R.I)
BEDROOM 2 (B.R.2)
BATHROOM (BATH)
1/2 BATHROOM (1/2BATH)
INTERIOR GARDEN (INT. GAR.)
KITCHEN (KIT.)

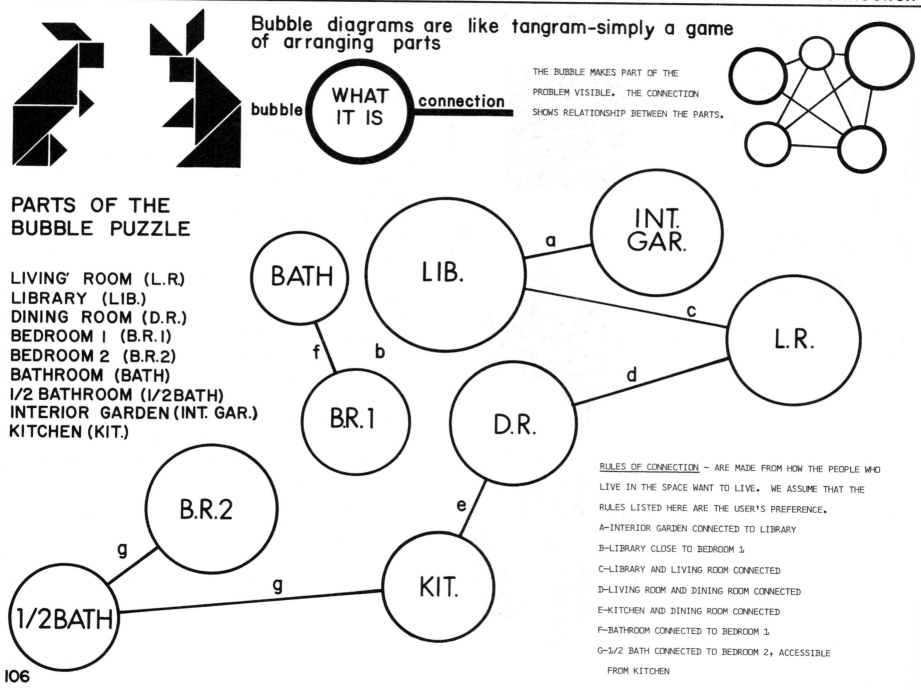

RULES OF CONNECTION — ARE MADE FROM HOW THE PEOPLE WHO LIVE IN THE SPACE WANT TO LIVE. WE ASSUME THAT THE RULES LISTED HERE ARE THE USER'S PREFERENCE.

A—INTERIOR GARDEN CONNECTED TO LIBRARY

B—LIBRARY CLOSE TO BEDROOM 1

C—LIBRARY AND LIVING ROOM CONNECTED

D—LIVING ROOM AND DINING ROOM CONNECTED

E—KITCHEN AND DINING ROOM CONNECTED

F—BATHROOM CONNECTED TO BEDROOM 1

G—1/2 BATH CONNECTED TO BEDROOM 2, ACCESSIBLE FROM KITCHEN

AS THE BUBBLES REPRESENTING
SPACES ARE CONNECTED, THE
DESIGNER MUST CONSIDER THEIR
OVERALL ARRANGEMENT. HOW WILL
THEY GO TOGETHER TO GIVE
PRIVACY, COMMUNITY, VIEW, AND
CONNECTION WITH THE COMMUNITY?

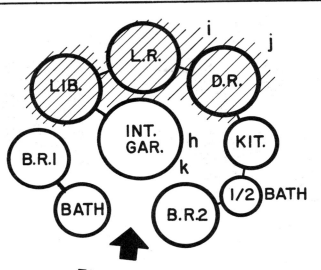

ENTRANCE

RULES OF ARRANGEMENT —

H—GARDEN IN THE CENTER OF THE HOUSE IS VIEWED FROM ALL INTERIOR
   SPACES.

I—LIVING AND SOCIAL SPACES AS REMOTE FROM THE STREET ENTRANCE
   AS POSSIBLE.

J—EXTERNAL VIEWS WITHOUT INTEREST EXCEPT FROM LIVING AND DINING
   ROOMS.

K—HOUSE TO BE AS COMPACT AS POSSIBLE WITH MAJOR INTEREST FOCUSED
   INTERNALLY UPON INTERIOR GARDEN.

AT THIS STAGE OF THE BUBBLE
DIAGRAM, THE SQUARE-FOOT AREAS
OF THE SPACES HAVE BEEN ESTIMATED.
BUBBLES BECOME SQUARES OF ROOM
AREA. THE OUTLINES OF THE FINAL
PLAN EMERGE. A CIRCULATION
CORRIDOR MUST BE ADDED TO MEET
THE RULES OF ARRANGEMENT.

ENTRANCE

THIS IS A VERY PRIVATE HOUSE THAT
SEEMS TO LOOK IN UPON ITSELF.

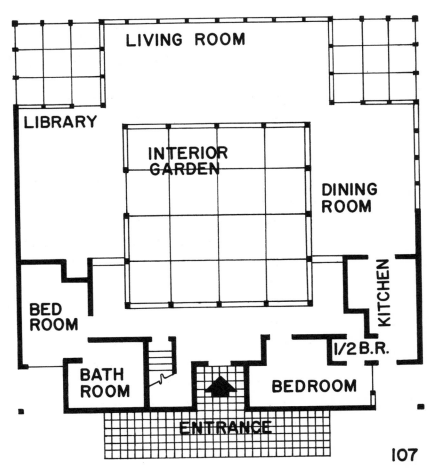

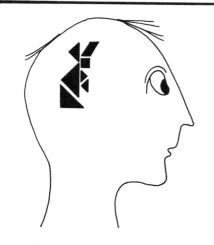

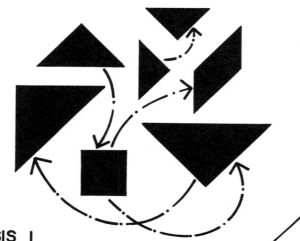

**SYNTHESIS**
PUTTING THE
PARTS TOGETHER

## ANALYSIS 1
WHAT ARE THE PARTS?
HOW DO THEY ASSEMBLE?

THE PUZZLE AS A PROBLEM—IN THIS METHOD OF THINKING OF THE TANS WE TRY TO ANALYZE THEIR BEST POSSIBLE COMBINATION BEFORE PUTTING THEM TOGETHER. ALTHOUGH LOGIC AND RATIONALITY ARE THE OBJECTIVES, INTUITION AND HUNCHES PLAY A PART.

THE PUZZLE-SOLVING PROCESS HAS THE ADVANTAGE OF IMMEDIATELY IN- VOLVING THE DESIGNER IN THE PROBLEM INSTEAD OF WAITING FOR INSPIRATION TO STRIKE, WHICH IS OFTEN A LONG WAIT.

METHOD—THE PUZZLE-PROBLEM METHOD INVOLVES 3 STEPS WHICH ARE REPEATED AS MANY TIMES AS IT TAKES TO ARRIVE AT A SATISFACTORY FIT BETWEEN THE PROBLEM AND THE SOLUTION.

    ANALYSIS        SYNTHESIS        EVALUATION

THERE IS ONE ESSENTIAL POINT TO REMEMBER. WE BEGIN WITH THE SOLUTION, WHICH IS A DEFINITION OF WHAT WE BELIEVE THE PROBLEM TO BE, AND ADJUST THE PARTS TO FIT. THIS IS THE OPPOSITE PROCEDURE TO OUR FIRST METHOD, WHICH WAS TO LET THE PARTS THEMSELVES SUGGEST A SOLUTION.

IN EACH REPETITION EACH ANALYSIS IS TEMPERED BY WHAT WAS LEARNED IN THE PREVIOUS SYNTHESIS AND EVALUATION.

**EVALUATION**
DO THE PARTS
FIT THE IDEA?

## ANALYSIS 2
REASSEMBLE THE
PARTS FOR A
BETTER FIT

THE PUZZLE-PROBLEM PROCEDURE MAKES A NUMBER OF GENERALIZATIONS ABOUT HOW PEOPLE ACT AS GROUPS. PEOPLE ARE NOT GENERALITIES. EACH IS AN EXCEPTION. ASSUMPTIONS MUST BE CONTINUALLY ADJUSTED.

## DEFINE THE PROBLEM

WE GIVE MEANING TO THE PROBLEM AT THE LEVEL OF UNDERSTANDING OF IT WE HAVE AT THE TIME. AS WE ANALYZE AND SYNTHESIZE WE ACQUIRE A CLEARER UNDERSTANDING, WHICH WILL INFLUENCE THE PROBLEM DEFINITION.

THE SOLUTION IS THE PHYSICAL TRANSLATION OF THE DEFINITION STATEMENT.

THE DEFINITION IS A SPECIFICATION OF DESIRED PERFORMANCE.

THE PROBLEM STATEMENT IS THE TRUTH AS FAR AS WE KNOW IT AT THE TIME, A TEMPORARY ULTIMATE GOAL.

## ANALYSIS

WHAT ARE THE LIMITS OF ADJUSTMENT?

WHAT CAN BE MOVED AND WHAT NOT?

WHAT CAN THE DESIGNER CONTROL AND WHAT NOT?

WHAT IS ALLOWED AND WHAT PROHIBITED?

## DESCRIPTION

PHYSICAL: COLOR, WEIGHT, MASS, SHAPE, SIZE.

PSYCHOLOGICAL: APPEARANCE, PERCEPTION, STIMULUS, SYMBOLISM.

SOCIAL: APPROVAL, RESPONSIBILITIES, POLITICAL, FUNCTIONAL.

OTHER: COST, FUNCTION, DURABILITY.

WE SIMPLY LIST ALL WE KNOW AND ALL WE CAN FIND OUT ABOUT THE PUZZLE ELEMENTS.

## SYNTHESIS

SELECT THE PARTS TO MINIMIZE THE CHOICES.

ASSIGN VALUES TO DECISIONS AND COMPARE.

ARRANGE ALTERNATIVES SO THAT THEY CAN BE CLEARLY UNDERSTOOD. COMPARE THE GOALS WITH THE MEANS OF ACHIEVING THEM.

WHAT DECISION WILL BEST BALANCE BENEFITS AND LIABILITIES?

## EVALUATION

COMPARE THE PROBLEM STATEMENT WITH THE SOLUTION.

FIND THE FAULTS.

COMPARE BENEFITS AND LIABILITIES.

TO EVALUATE AND TEST THE SOLUTION, IT IS OFTEN HELPFUL TO MANIPULATE PARTS OF THE SOLUTION TO FIND HOW A CHANGE IN A PART WILL EFFECT THE WHOLE.

IN THE END, THE FINAL DESIGN WILL BE THE RESULT OF A SERIES OF EXCHANGES OR COMPROMISES AND COMPARISONS INVOLVING ALL THE ELEMENTS OF THE PROBLEM.

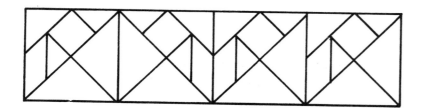

INTERIOR SPACE IS CREATED BY EXTERIOR SHELLS OVER WHICH THE INTERIOR DESIGNER EXERCISES LITTLE CONTROL. AS A CONSEQUENCE THERE ARE THREE DESIGN POSSIBILITIES, TO DESIGN WITH, TO DESIGN AGAINST THE SPACE, OR TO CONTINUE WHAT THE ARCHITECT HAS LEFT UNFINISHED.

THE ROOMS OF A WELL-DESIGNED BUILDING ARRANGE THEMSELVES. THEY SUGGEST HOW THE ROOM IS TO BE USED BY THEIR CONTROL OF LIGHT, VENTILATION, HUMAN MOVEMENT, AND OTHER SUBTLE AND OBVIOUS DIRECTIVES. ON THE OTHER HAND, THE SPACES OF ANONYMOUS CURTAIN-WALL OFFICE BUILDINGS GIVE NO CLUES AT ALL. MOST INTERIOR DESIGN PROBLEMS FALL SOMEWHERE IN BETWEEN THESE TWO EXTREMES.

PUZZLE-PROBLEM GENERAL STATEMENT—THE ROOM TO BE DESIGNED IS THE LIVING ROOM OF A FORMER PRIVATE DWELLING THAT IS BEING CONVERTED TO AN INFORMAL CONFERENCE AND SOCIAL MEETING CENTER FOR THE STAFF OF A SMALL NURSERY SCHOOL.

PROBLEM ANALYSIS—HOW MANY PEOPLE WILL USE THE SPACE AND HOW WILL THEY SIT, STAND, READ, CONVERSE, IN SMALL OR LARGE GROUPS? AT WHAT TIME OF THE DAY WILL THE ROOM BE USED? WILL THEY USE IT ALL AT ONCE OR TWO OR THREE AT A TIME? WHAT MOOD SHOULD THE SPACE EVOKE: SERIOUS, PLAYFUL, DIGNIFIED, OR CASUAL?

WHAT KIND OF FURNITURE IS NEEDED. WHAT ARE THE POSSIBLE MOVEMENT PATTERNS. WHAT SHOULD THE ACOUSTIC ENVIRONMENT BE. WHAT KIND OF LIGHTING IS REQUIRED.

FROM THESE INQUIRIES, THE DESIGNER GATHERS INFORMATION ABOUT THE PROBLEM AND FURTHER DEFINES IT. THE PROBLEM STATEMENT BECOMES PARTICULAR AND DETAILED.

THE INFORMATION IS THEN TRANSLATED INTO POSSIBLE SOLUTIONS BY MEANS OF DRAWINGS WHICH COMBINE THE REQUIREMENTS DEFINED IN ANALYSIS. THE INFORMATION IS PUT TOGETHER, SYNTHESIZED, AND COMPARED TO THE PROBLEM STATEMENT WHICH IS THE EVALUATION.

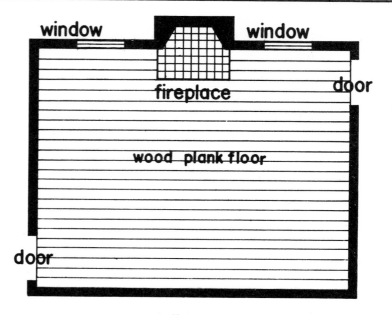

## ROOM PLAN

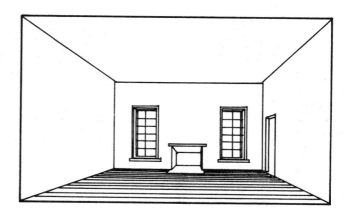

## PERSPECTIVE VIEW OF ROOM

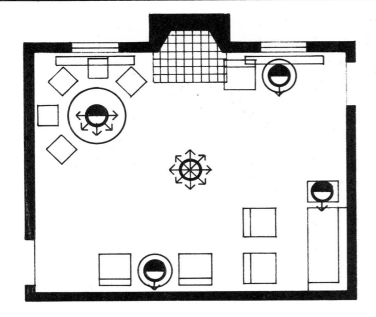

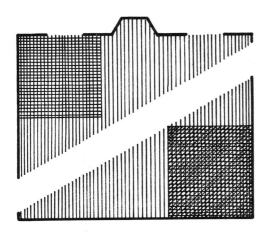

## ZONES OF PRIVACY

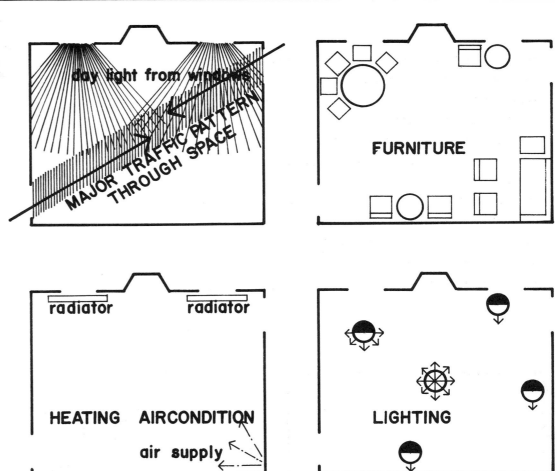

day light from windows

MAJOR TRAFFIC PATTERN THROUGH SPACE

**FURNITURE**

radiator          radiator

**HEATING  AIRCONDITION**

air supply

**LIGHTING**

DRAW THE PLAN OUTLINES OF THE ROOM IN INK OR HEAVY PENCIL. DRAW TO SCALE
OR ON GRAPH PAPER. DRAW THE WALLS, DOOR, AND WINDOW OPENINGS, AND ROOM
FEATURES THAT CANNOT BE CHANGED.

LAY TISSUE PAPER OVER THE PLAN. DRAW THE FURNITURE ARRANGEMENT. TAKE
ANOTHER SHEET OF TISSUE PAPER AND DRAW TRAFFIC PATTERNS. ANOTHER SHEET IS
NEEDED FOR LIGHT, BOTH ARTIFICIAL AND DAYLIGHT, AND ONE FOR AIR CIRCULATION.

WHEN YOU HAVE GRAPHICALLY ANALYZED EACH INTERIOR DESIGN ELEMENT INDIVI-
DUALLY, TAKE THE VARIOUS SHEETS AND LAY THEM OVER THE ORIGINAL PLAN.

# ORTHOGRAPHIC DRAWING

DRAWING, FROM ROUGH SKETCHES TO FINISHED RENDERINGS, ARE THE LANGUAGE THE INTERIOR DESIGNER USES TO CONVEY IDEAS TO OTHERS AND TO THINK THEM OUT FOR HIMSELF.

EVENTUALLY EVERY DESIGNER DEVELOPS HIS OWN UNIQUE GRAPHIC LANGUAGE, WHICH IS USUALLY A COMBINATION OF A NUMBER OF TECHNIQUES. THE METHODS SHOWN HERE ARE TRADITIONAL DRAFTING TECHNIQUES USED BY ARCHITECTS AND BUILDERS.

ORTHOGRAPHIC PROJECTION—PLAN, SECTION, AND ELEVATIONS ARE DRAWN AS IF THEY WERE PERPENDICULAR TO THE OBSERVER'S LINE OF SIGHT WITHOUT PERSPECTIVE. ALL DETAILS OF THE FORM ARE DRAWN PARALLEL TO THE DRAWING SURFACE AND SHOWN WITHOUT FORESHORTENING OR DISTORTION. THEY RETAIN THEIR TRUE SIZE AND ARE DRAWN AT THE SCALE SELECTED.

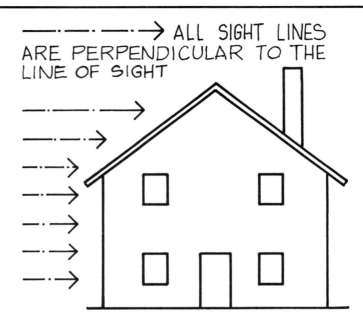

ALL SIGHT LINES ARE PERPENDICULAR TO THE LINE OF SIGHT

ELEVATION—THE FRONT VIEW OF THE OBJECT.

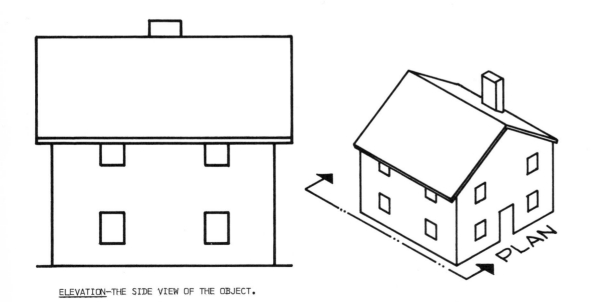

ELEVATION—THE SIDE VIEW OF THE OBJECT.

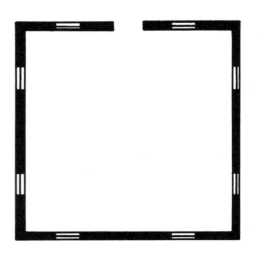

PLAN—A HORIZONTAL SECTION. DRAWN AS IF THE OBJECT HAD BEEN CUT THROUGH AND WE WERE LOOKING DOWN.

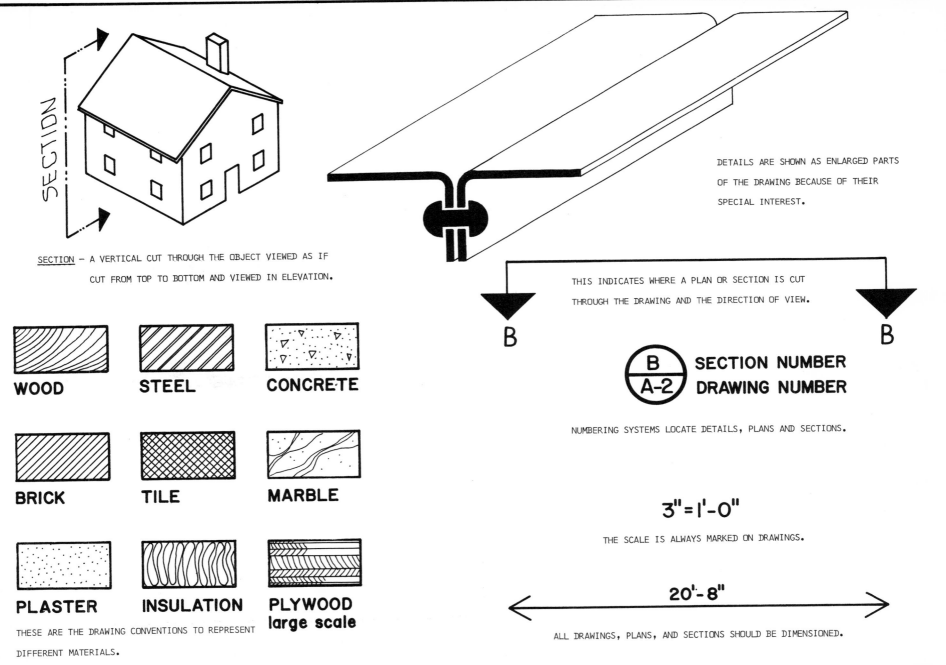

SECTION

SECTION – A VERTICAL CUT THROUGH THE OBJECT VIEWED AS IF
CUT FROM TOP TO BOTTOM AND VIEWED IN ELEVATION.

DETAILS ARE SHOWN AS ENLARGED PARTS
OF THE DRAWING BECAUSE OF THEIR
SPECIAL INTEREST.

**WOOD**  **STEEL**  **CONCRETE**

**BRICK**  **TILE**  **MARBLE**

**PLASTER**  **INSULATION**  **PLYWOOD**
**large scale**

THESE ARE THE DRAWING CONVENTIONS TO REPRESENT
DIFFERENT MATERIALS.

THIS INDICATES WHERE A PLAN OR SECTION IS CUT
THROUGH THE DRAWING AND THE DIRECTION OF VIEW.

B          B

B / A-2   **SECTION NUMBER**
          **DRAWING NUMBER**

NUMBERING SYSTEMS LOCATE DETAILS, PLANS AND SECTIONS.

$$3"=1'-0"$$

THE SCALE IS ALWAYS MARKED ON DRAWINGS.

←———— 20'-8" ————→

ALL DRAWINGS, PLANS, AND SECTIONS SHOULD BE DIMENSIONED.

# ISOMETRIC AND OBLIQUE DRAWING

THERE ARE METHODS OF MAKING DRAWINGS IN WHICH ALL VERTICAL LINES REMAIN
VERTICAL AND ALL PARALLEL LINES REMAIN PARALLEL.  ALL LINES CAN BE DRAWN
TO SCALE.  THE DRAWINGS SEEM SLIGHTLY DISTORTED BUT THEY GIVE THE
APPEARANCE OF PERSPECTIVE.  THREE SIDES OF THE OBJECT ARE SHOWN, AND THE
METHOD IS SIMPLE AND EFFICIENT.

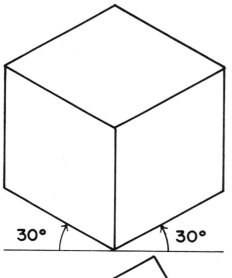

**ISOMETRIC—**
ALL THREE VISIBLE
SURFACES HAVE EQUAL
EMPHASIS.

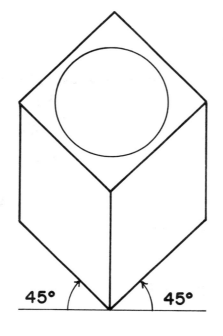

**OBLIQUE  45—45 —**
A HIGHER ANGLE OF VIEW THAN
THE ISOMETRIC.  THE HORIZONTAL
PLANES HAVE MORE EMPHASIS.
THE ANGLE AT TOP IS 90 DEGREES.
TRUE CIRCLES CAN BE USED.

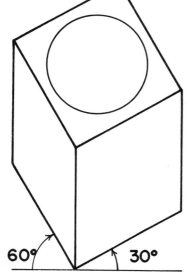

**OBLIQUE 60—30 —**
THE TOP PLANE RECEIVES
EMPHASIS AND ONE SIDE IS
MORE PRONOUNCED THAN THE
OTHER.  TRUE CIRCLES CAN
BE DRAWN ON THE
HORIZONTAL PLANE.

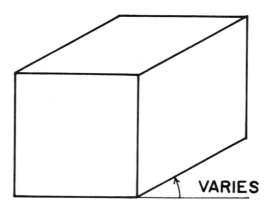

**ELEVATION OBLIQUE —**
VERTICAL PLANE REMAINS
PARALLEL TO DRAWING
SURFACE.  SIDE ANGLES
CAN BE VARIED.

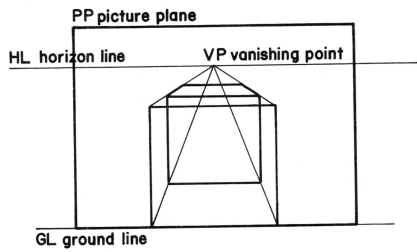

**PP picture plane**

**HL horizon line**    **VP vanishing point**

**GL ground line**

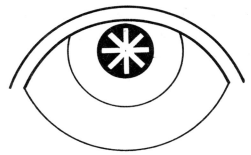

## STATION POINT

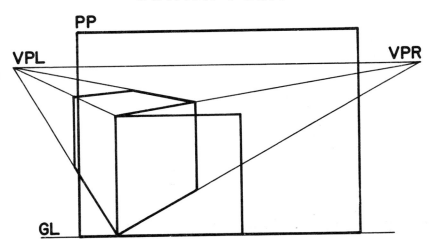

**PP**

**VPL**          **VPR**

**GL**

PERSPECTIVE DRAWING ELIMINATES THE OPTICAL DISTORTION OF LINES DRAWN PARALLEL AND PRESENTS THE OPTICAL ILLUSION OF FORM IN THREE DIMENSIONS. THE THEORY OF PERSPECTIVE DRAWING IS QUITE COMPLEX. THE METHODS SHOWN HERE ARE SHORT CUTS. AS THESE SIMPLE TECHNIQUES ARE USED, SKILL WILL DEVELOP UNTIL PERSPECTIVE LINES CAN BE DRAWN FREEHAND.

PERSPECTIVE DRAWINGS HAVE FOUR MAJOR CHARACTERISTICS THAT CREATE A SENSE OF SPACE, DEPTH, AND VOLUME: 1—FORMS OVERLAP; 2—FORMS REDUCE IN SIZE AS THEY MOVE AWAY FROM THE OBSERVER; 3—PARALLEL LINES CONVERGE INTO THE DISTANCE; AND 4—LINES ARE FORESHORTENED.

HL/HORIZON LINE— ALL LINES AS THEY RECEDE SEEM TO COME DOWN OR UP TO THE LEVEL OF THE OBSERVER'S EYES.

PP/PICTURE PLANE— AN IMAGINARY TRANSPARENT PLANE PLACED BETWEEN THE OBSERVER AND THE SUBJECT. TRUE DIMENSIONS ARE MEASURED ON THIS PLANE WHEN CONSTRUCTING A PERSPECTIVE DRAWING.

SP/STATION POINT— THE OBSERVER'S EYES ARE THE POINT OF VIEW FROM WHICH THE PERSPECTIVE ORIGINATES.

GL/GROUND LINE— THE LINE UPON WHICH THE PICTURE PLANE RESTS.

VP/VPI/VPR/VANISHING POINT, LEFT AND RIGHT— THE POINT AT WHICH LINES SEEM TO CONVERGE ON THE HORIZON LINE AS THEY COME TO THE HEIGHT OF THE OBSERVER'S EYES, OR THE SP.

MP/MPL/MPR/MEASURING POINT, LEFT AND RIGHT— THE POINT USED TO ESTABLISH THE MEASUREMENTS IN A MEASURED PERSPECTIVE.

# ONE-POINT PERSPECTIVE

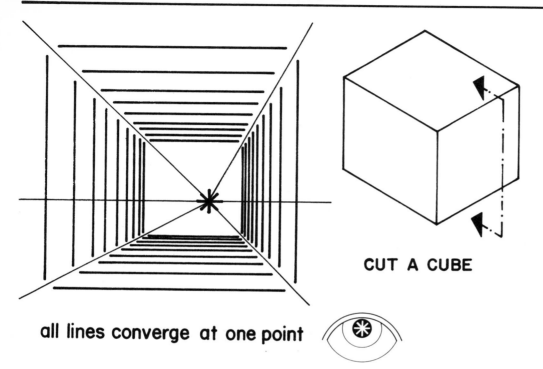

**all lines converge at one point**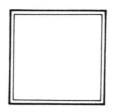

**CUT A CUBE**

**ORTHOGRAPHIC DRAWING
FRONT AND SIDE VIEWS**

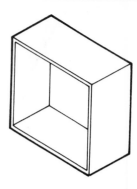

**ISOMETRIC**

ORTHOGRAPHIC DRAWINGS SHOW ONE VIEW AT A TIME.   THE ISOMETRIC
SHOWS MORE BUT THE VIEW IS DISTORTED.   A ONE-POINT PERSPECTIVE
WILL SHOW THE CUBE'S INTERIOR AS IT WOULD ACTUALLY APPEAR, OR
AT LEAST AS CLOSE TO REALITY AS THE OPTICAL ILLUSION OF PERS-
PECTIVE CAN PROVIDE.

**the cube is cut at the picture plane**

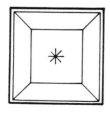 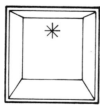 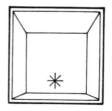 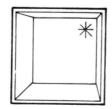 

**that is an important point-what is seen in the cubes interior depends upon it**

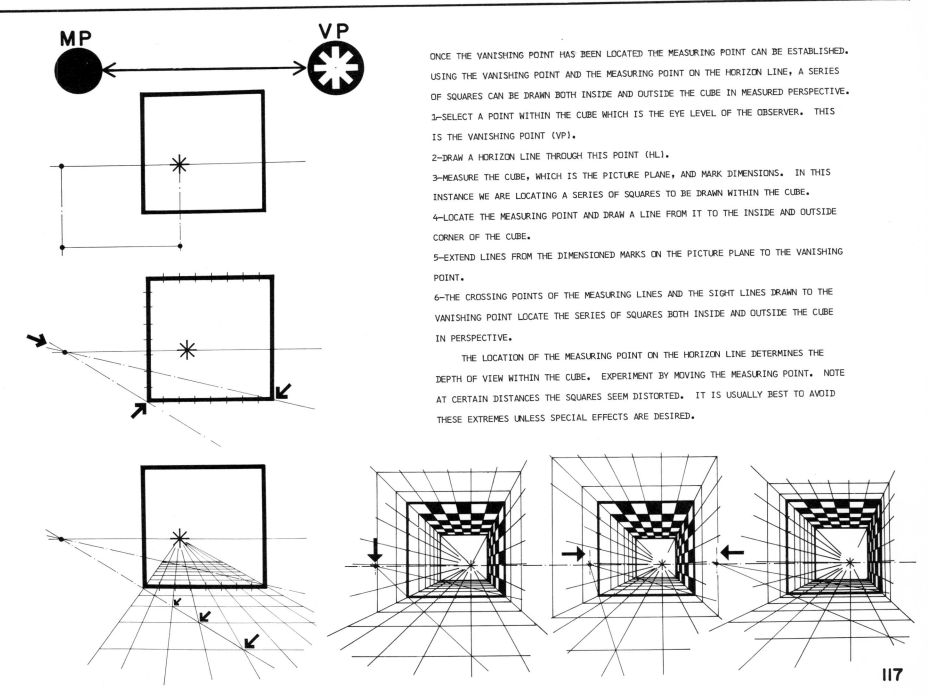

ONCE THE VANISHING POINT HAS BEEN LOCATED THE MEASURING POINT CAN BE ESTABLISHED.
USING THE VANISHING POINT AND THE MEASURING POINT ON THE HORIZON LINE, A SERIES
OF SQUARES CAN BE DRAWN BOTH INSIDE AND OUTSIDE THE CUBE IN MEASURED PERSPECTIVE.

1—SELECT A POINT WITHIN THE CUBE WHICH IS THE EYE LEVEL OF THE OBSERVER. THIS
IS THE VANISHING POINT (VP).

2—DRAW A HORIZON LINE THROUGH THIS POINT (HL).

3—MEASURE THE CUBE, WHICH IS THE PICTURE PLANE, AND MARK DIMENSIONS. IN THIS
INSTANCE WE ARE LOCATING A SERIES OF SQUARES TO BE DRAWN WITHIN THE CUBE.

4—LOCATE THE MEASURING POINT AND DRAW A LINE FROM IT TO THE INSIDE AND OUTSIDE
CORNER OF THE CUBE.

5—EXTEND LINES FROM THE DIMENSIONED MARKS ON THE PICTURE PLANE TO THE VANISHING
POINT.

6—THE CROSSING POINTS OF THE MEASURING LINES AND THE SIGHT LINES DRAWN TO THE
VANISHING POINT LOCATE THE SERIES OF SQUARES BOTH INSIDE AND OUTSIDE THE CUBE
IN PERSPECTIVE.

THE LOCATION OF THE MEASURING POINT ON THE HORIZON LINE DETERMINES THE
DEPTH OF VIEW WITHIN THE CUBE. EXPERIMENT BY MOVING THE MEASURING POINT. NOTE
AT CERTAIN DISTANCES THE SQUARES SEEM DISTORTED. IT IS USUALLY BEST TO AVOID
THESE EXTREMES UNLESS SPECIAL EFFECTS ARE DESIRED.

# TWO-POINT PERSPECTIVE

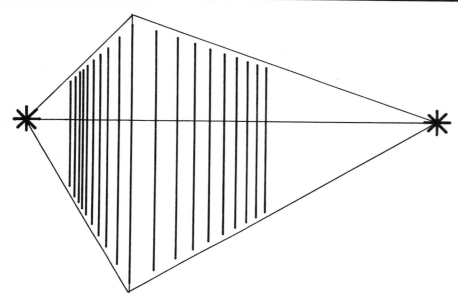

### all lines converge at two points

TO CONSTRUCT A GRID OF SQUARES IN PERSPECTIVE FOR TWO VANISHING POINTS
FOLLOW THIS PROCEDURE:

1—DRAW A HORIZON LINE.

2—USING A 30-60 DEGREE TRIANGLE, DRAW TWO LINES OF 30 AND 60 DEGREES CONVERGING
BELOW THE HORIZON LINE.  THE TWO VANISHING POINTS (VPR,VPL) ARE LOCATED WHERE
THE 30-60 LINES TOUCH THE HORIZON LINE.

3—DRAW A GROUND LINE WHERE THE LINES CONVERGE.  THIS IS ALSO THE MEASURING LINE.

4—MARK OFF ON THE HORIZON LINE A DISTANCE EQUAL TO THE DISTANCE FROM THE GL TO
VPR.  THIS IS MPR.  DO THE SAME FOR GL TO VPL TO LOCATE MPL.

5—DRAW A VERTICAL LINE FROM THE INTERSECTION OF THE 30-60 LINES UPWARD.  THIS
WILL BE THE VERTICAL MEASURING LINE.

ALL TRUE MEASUREMENTS CAN BE LOCATED ON THE VERTICAL LINE AND THE GROUND
LINE.  FROM THESE A GRID OF SQUARES IN PERSPECTIVE CAN BE CONSTRUCTED IN WHICH
IT IS POSSIBLE TO DRAW OBJECTS IN TWO-POINT PERSPECTIVE.

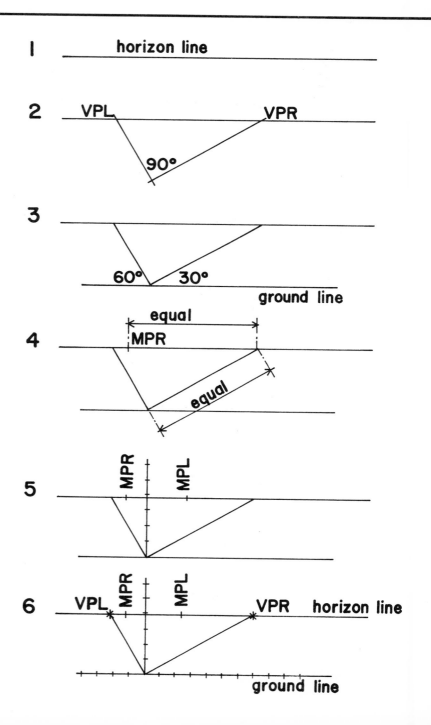

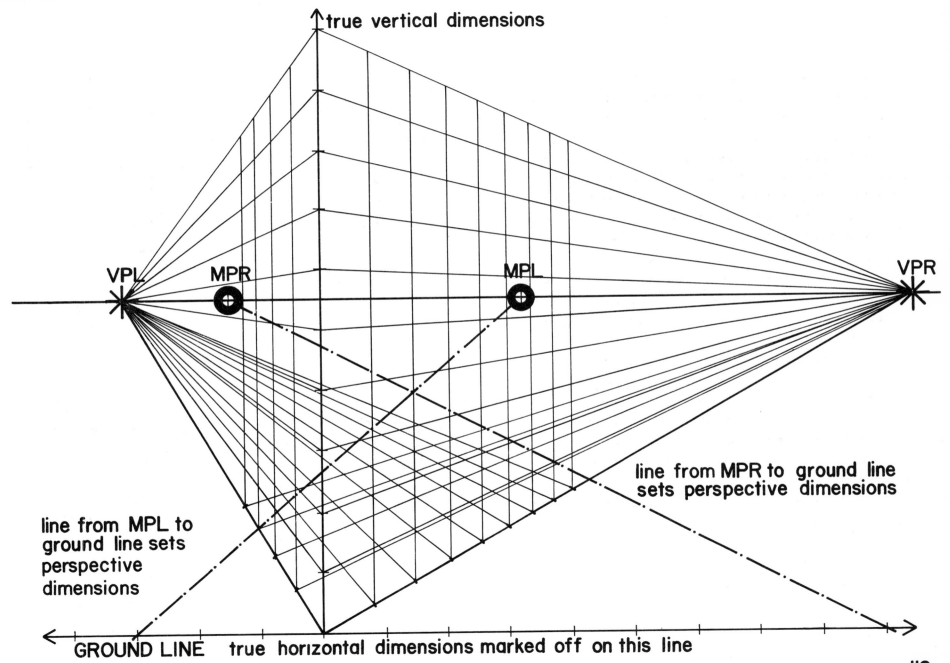

true vertical dimensions

VPL   MPR   MPL   VPR

line from MPR to ground line
sets perspective dimensions

line from MPL to
ground line sets
perspective
dimensions

GROUND LINE   true horizontal dimensions marked off on this line

MODELS PRESENT THE DESIGN IN MINIATURE. OF THE TWO KINDS OF MODELS CONSTRUCTED, THE FIRST ARE MODELS DESIGNERS MAKE FOR THEMSELVES FOR STUDY AND THE SECOND ARE MODELS DESIGNERS MAKE FOR THEIR CLIENTS. THE DIFFERENCE IS THE AMOUNT OF WORK AND THE VALUE OF THE MATERIALS IN EACH MODEL.

STUDY MODELS ARE MADE OF ROUGH MATERIALS, LOOKED AT FOR A SHORT TIME AND THEN DISCARDED. CLIENT MODELS ARE CAREFULLY CONSTRUCTED OF EXPENSIVE MATERIALS AND USED FOR DISPLAY OR AS MOMENTOES FOR LONG PERIODS OF TIME.

FULL-SIZED MODELS OF FURNITURE OR INTERIOR DETAILS ARE SOMETIMES MADE BUT USUALLY MODELS ARE MADE SMALLER. ACTUAL SIZE IS REDUCED PROPORTIONATELY WITH A SCALE RULE. THESE RULES ARE MARKED IN SIZES PROPORTIONATELY TO FULL SIZE. FOR EXAMPLE, IF WE USE A SCALE OF 3 INCHES EQUALS 1 FOOT, EVERY INCH ON THE SCALE RULE EQUALS 4 INCHES AND EVERY 1/4 INCH EQUALS 1 INCH. THIS IS A VERY LARGE SCALE AND IS USUALLY USED ONLY WHEN THE DESIGNER WISHES TO STUDY COMPLEX DETAILS.

A MORE USUAL SCALE WOULD BE 1 INCH EQUALS 1 FOOT, IN WHICH EVERY 1/4 INCH EQUALS 3 INCHES. THE LARGER THE OBJECT STUDIES, THE SMALLER THE SCALE. SMALL SCALES SUCH AS 1/4, 1/8 OR EVEN 1/16 INCH ARE SOMETIMES USED.

TO MAKE A STUDY MODEL THE DESIGNER SIMPLY DRAWS HIS DESIGN TO SCALE ON CARDBOARD OR HEAVY DRAFTING PAPER, CUTS OUT THE PARTS AND GLUES THEM TOGETHER. THE OBJECTIVE IS TO CREATE A THREE-DIMENSIONAL SKETCH OF THE IDEA TO CLARIFY DESIGN CONCEPTS.

A PHOTOGRAPH OF A PERSON OR A DRAWING TO THE RIGHT SCALE CUT OUT AND PASTED ON CARDBOARD AND PLACED IN THE MODEL OR NEXT TO IT GIVES A REALISTIC APPEARANCE WHICH IS HELPFUL IN ESTABLISHING THE SCALE OF HUMAN BEINGS.

HOBBY SHOPS OR HARDWARE, ART, AND STATIONERY STORES SELL TOOLS AND MATERIALS NEEDED FOR MODEL-MAKING.

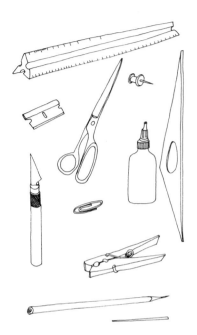

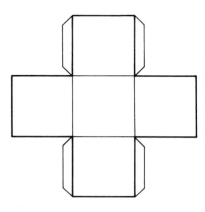

**BASIC BOX**

BASIC BOX

a design tool

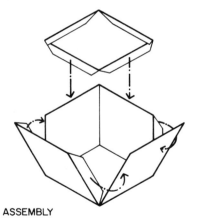

ASSEMBLY

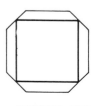

OPTIONAL TOP

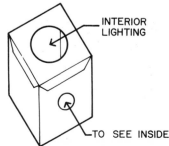

INTERIOR LIGHTING

TO SEE INSIDE

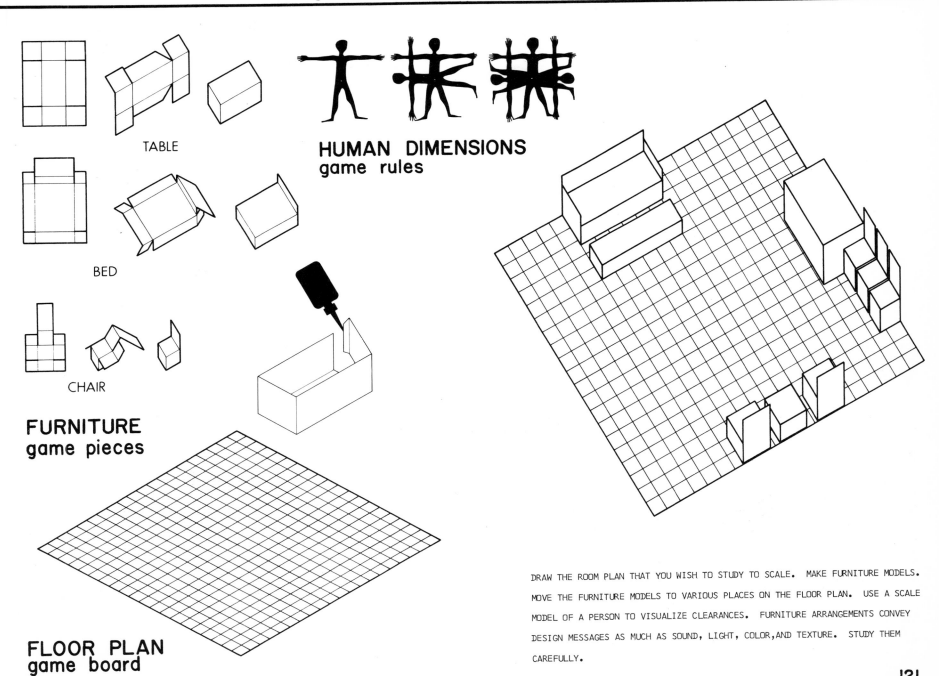

TABLE

BED

CHAIR

**HUMAN DIMENSIONS**
game rules

**FURNITURE**
game pieces

**FLOOR PLAN**
game board

DRAW THE ROOM PLAN THAT YOU WISH TO STUDY TO SCALE. MAKE FURNITURE MODELS.
MOVE THE FURNITURE MODELS TO VARIOUS PLACES ON THE FLOOR PLAN. USE A SCALE
MODEL OF A PERSON TO VISUALIZE CLEARANCES. FURNITURE ARRANGEMENTS CONVEY
DESIGN MESSAGES AS MUCH AS SOUND, LIGHT, COLOR, AND TEXTURE. STUDY THEM
CAREFULLY.

121

# THE VIEW FROM YOUR FINGERS

RASPY VOICE   HARD NOSE

COTTON MOUTH

SOFT HEARTED

LIGHT FINGERED

HEAVY HANDED

FUZZY THINKING

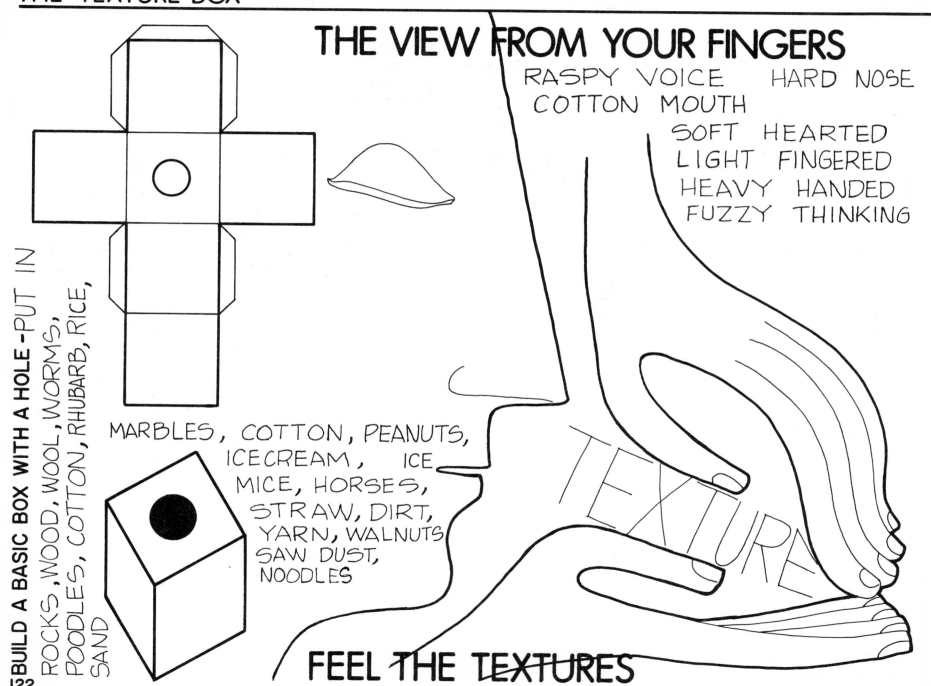

**BUILD A BASIC BOX WITH A HOLE** - PUT IN

ROCKS, WOOD, WOOL, WORMS, POODLES, COTTON, RHUBARB, RICE, SAND

MARBLES, COTTON, PEANUTS, ICECREAM, ICE MICE, HORSES, STRAW, DIRT, YARN, WALNUTS SAW DUST, NOODLES

# FEEL THE TEXTURES

# SEEING WITH SOUND

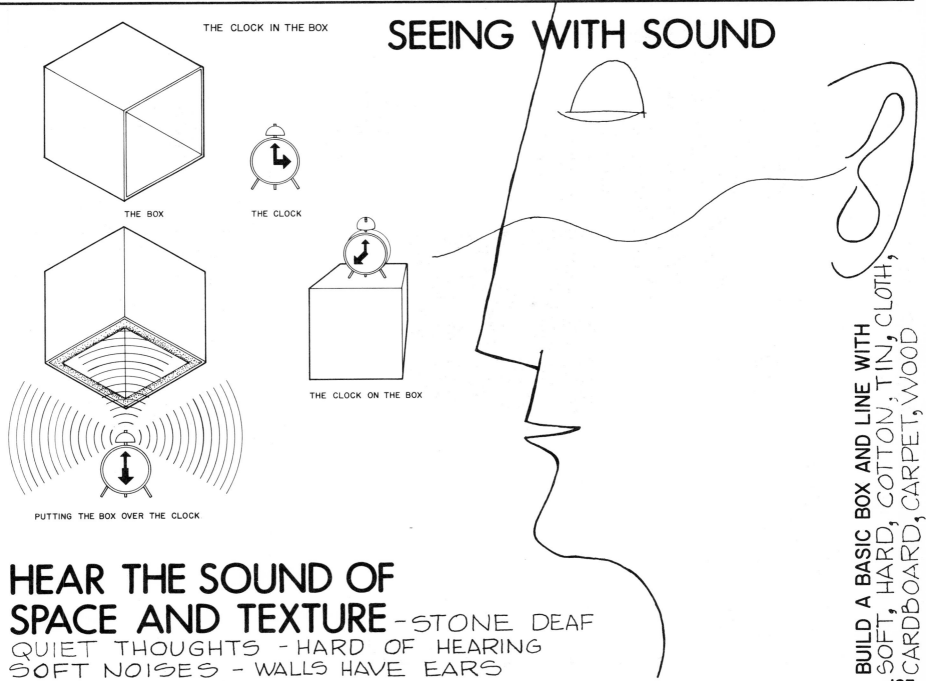

THE CLOCK IN THE BOX

THE BOX

THE CLOCK

THE CLOCK ON THE BOX

PUTTING THE BOX OVER THE CLOCK

# HEAR THE SOUND OF
# SPACE AND TEXTURE - STONE DEAF
QUIET THOUGHTS - HARD OF HEARING
SOFT NOISES - WALLS HAVE EARS

BUILD A BASIC BOX AND LINE WITH
SOFT, HARD, COTTON, TIN, CLOTH,
CARDBOARD, CARPET, WOOD

BASIC BOX WITH PATTERNS

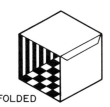

FOLDED

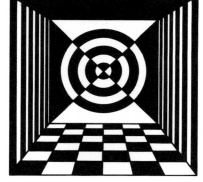

LOOKING INSIDE

**DRAW PATTERNS INSIDE OF A BASIC BOX**
SHORTEN, LENGTHEN
THE WALLS, DROP
THE CEILING, RAISE
THE ROOF, ADD
PERSPECTIVE
EMPHASIZE
DESTROY THE
CUBE

STEELY VISION,
BEDROOM EYES,
POINT OF VIEW,
TUNNEL VISION,
SEE WHAT
YOU MEAN,
RIVET THE
EYES,
VIEW POINT,
SEE RED, SHARP
VISION, A SIGHT
FOR SORE EYES

SEEING is BELIEVING

# NOW YOU SEE IT
# NOW YOU DON'T

THE ROOM AS A BASIC
BOX TO STUDY
LIGHT

WINDOW OPENINGS

TO SEE INSIDE

THE ROOM AS A BOX

TOP OF THE BOX

SUN

THE ROOM BOX ON A WINDOW SILL

OPENINGS IN TOP FOR
ARTIFICIAL LIGHT

# LIGHT TRANSFORMS

BUILD A BOX TO THE SCALE OF THE ROOM - CUT OPENINGS
FOR WINDOWS AND OPENINGS FOR ARTIFICIAL LIGHT
PUT THE BOX WHERE THE LIGHT IS - LOOK INSIDE

# CONCLUSION

ARISTOTLE CALLED WORK INTELLIGENT ACTION.  DESIGN SEEMS TO BE SIMPLY THE
INTELLIGENCE IN THE ACTION OF WORK.  DESIGN WITHOUT WORK IS MERELY A
THEORY OF HOW THINGS SHOULD BE DONE.  WORK WITHOUT DESIGN IS UGLY DRUDGERY.

THE BUILDINGS OF INSECTS AND ANIMALS ARE OFTEN FAR SUPERIOR TO THOSE
OF HUMANS IN STRUCTURE, COMFORT, AND CONVENIENCE.  THE DIFFERENCE BETWEEN
THE MOST INGENIOUS INSECT AND THE CLUMSIEST HUMAN BUILDER IS SIMPLY THAT
WE CAN PLAN OUR WORK IN OUR MINDS BEFORE WE BUILD WITH OUR HANDS AND ARE
THEREFORE CAPABLE OF DESIGN.  IT IS THIS THAT DISTINGUISHES THE WORK OF
HUMANS FROM INSECTS, BIRDS, AND AARDVARKS.  HUMANS DESIGN; ANIMALS SIMPLY
BUILD.

NEITHER OUR INSTINCTS NOR OUR SENSES ARE AS WELL DEVELOPED AS THOSE
OF ANIMALS.  BUT  WE CAN ANALYZE OUR INSTINCTS INSTEAD OF FOLLOWING THEM
BLINDLY AND DEVELOP OUR SENSES TO ALERT US TO THINGS OTHER THAN SEX, FOOD,
AND DANGER.

FEELINGS OF WELL-BEING, FRUSTRATION, PLEASURE, EXCITEMENT, AND BOREDOM
ORIGINATE IN OUR SENSES OF SIGHT, HEARING, SMELL, TASTE, AND TOUCH.  THESE
ARE THINGS THAT NO ONE ELSE CAN DO FOR US.  WE CANNOT SEE THROUGH ANOTHER'S
EYES, HEAR THROUGH THEIR EARS, SMELL THROUGH THEIR NOSE, TASTE WITH THEIR
TASTE BUDS OR EXPERIENCE A FEELING OF TEXTURE WITH THEIR FINGERS.

THERE CAN BE NO OTHER REAL EXPERTS ON HOW WE FEEL, THAN OURSELVES.
THEREFORE, THIS BOOK MAY NOT TELL YOU ANYTHING YOU DID NOT ALREADY HAVE THE
SENSES TO FIND OUT FOR YOURSELF.  IF YOU HAVE LEARNED THIS, IT HAS BEEN WORTH
MY WRITING AND YOUR READING.

# INDEX

# INDEX